THE WORLD
OF THE MYSTIC

THE WORLD OF THE MYSTIC

by
Samuel Umen

Philosophical Library
New York

Library of Congress Cataloging-in-Publication Data

Umen, Samuel.
  The world of the mystic.

  Bibliography: p.
  Includes index.
  1. Mysticism—Comparative studies. I. Title.
BL625.U45   1987   291.4'2   87-2257
ISBN 0-8022-2531-4

Copyright 1988 by Philosophical Library, Inc.
200 West 57th Street, New York, N.Y. 10019

Dedicated
To
His Eminence
Bernard Cardinal Law
A man of love and understanding,
a genuine human being,
a true representative of his faith.

Contents

Preface

People who have never been exposed to a study of mysticism have strange notions about the subject. Some believe it to be a form of knowledge by which magic can be performed, and its performer they call by the name of mystic.

Others, who are misinformed on the subject, consider mysticism as some kind of a secret formula which enables its possessor to communicate with the spirits of the dead.

Still others, due to sheer ignorance, regard mysticism as a doctrine which causes its adherents to behave strangely. The erroneous perceptions of mysticism are multitudinous. But since we are all mystics to a degree without being conscious of it, it behooves us to gain an understanding of mysticism based not on imaginings but on genuine information.

Out of fairness to the subject of mysticism, so terribly misunderstood by so many, and out of equal fairness to the mystic, who is no less misunderstood, I present this book, which simply and clearly defines mysticism and vividly depicts the mystic in his various states of mind, his struggle to attain his life's goal, which is to satisfy his soul's hunger of uniting with the Absolute, the Source of its being.

At the same time, the book affords the reader a faithful picture of the mystic in the context of his or her particular religion, such as Hinduism, Buddhism, Judaism, Christianity, and Islamism.

Once the reader properly acquaints himself or herself through the pages of this book with the meaning of mysticism and the particular life of the mystic, he or she will simultaneously gain a deeper understanding of himself or herself and will also come to realize how much or how little he or she is in accord with the mystic's goal and why.

S.U.

Acknowledgments

To my beloved wife, Lenore, for her many helpful suggestions in preparing the manuscript, I offer my heartfelt thanks.

To Jacqueline Hickox, Humanities secretary at New Hampshire College, where I teach philosophy, for taking time out from her pressing and demanding schedule to lovingly type my manuscript, I am profoundly thankful.

To my colleague Dr. Don Sieker, one of the most outstanding English scholars at New Hampshire College, I am deeply indebted for the honor he paid me by carefully reviewing the manuscript, and by mercilessly using his scalpel in eradicating all the errors he found therein.

To Dr. Max Stackhouse, Professor of Christian Social Ethics at Andover Newton Seminary; Reverend Placidus Riley, Professor of Theology at St. Anselm College; Dr. Eugene Mihaly, Professor of Rabbinic Literature and Homiletics at Hebrew Union College-Jewish Institute of Religion; and His Excellency Joseph J. Gerry, the Auxiliary Bishop of the Manchester, New Hampshire Diocese, all busy individuals with their own special charges, who were kind enough to read my work and offer their reactions to it which appear in part on the back of the book jacket, I offer my profuse gratitude.

S.U.

Introduction

There are certain people in the world who claim that the sense-world is unreal and that true Reality lies behind the world of our senses.

If one were to ask these special individuals what the basis is for their conclusion, where they obtained their information on the matter of Real and unreal Reality, their answer no doubt would be: "We speak from actual experience. We have been to the Real world. We have compared and know the difference between the two realities.

"In the sense-world, the illusory, unreal world, man is restless, confused, disturbed, insecure, and despite all his material possessions is unhappy and is dreaming of a more ideal condition. The Real world, on the other hand, offers the dweller a feeling of peace, a feeling of security. In this world, we find neither hate, jealousy, envy, fear; nor are there race problems, national disagreements, or religious differences.

"In the Real world, we feel as if we had been away on an extended, tiring journey, and at long last have come home."

Again, if one were to ask any of the special people how to get to what they term the Real world, the answer would be that the procedure is not an easy one. It entails much effort and sacrifice. It calls for relinquishing one's interest in pursuits of a material nature (that is, the acquisition of things), adopting a new standard for one's life and adjusting mentally to a new outlook on the universe.

If, before starting on his way to the Real world, one would press any of these special people for some more information about the true world, which perhaps was withheld from him through oversight, the answer would be this: "All the words available to us to describe our world to you have been completely exhausted. For you to know more about it now, you must personally experience it.

"The Real world we tried to tell you about is the one in which man merges with Divine Reality; he becomes one with the Source. No person has the capacity to translate this unutterable feeling into words."

Now, who are these special people who claim to have discovered true Reality? These people are often referred to as the adventurers of the Spirit. They are the mystics of our world and mysticism is the means by which they transcend the world of matter and reach the true world. These special people have appeared in every period of history, in every land and every clime.

"They are the heroic examples of the life of spirit; as the great artists, the great discoverers, are the heroic examples of the life of beauty and the life of truth. Directly participating like all artists, in the Divine Life, they are usually persons of great vitality; but this vitality expresses itself in unusual forms, hard of understanding for ordinary men. When we see a picture or a poem, hear a musical composition, we accept it as an expression of life, an earnest of the power which brought it forth. But the deep contemplations of the great mystic, his visionary reconstructions of reality, and the fragments of them which he is able to report do not seem to us—as they are—the equivalents, or more often the superiors, of the artistic and scientific achievements of other great men.

"Mysticism, then, offers us the history, as old as civilization, of a race of adventurers who have carried to its term the process of a deliberate and active return to the divine fount of things. They have surrendered themselves, to the life-movement of the universe, hence have lived with an intenser life than other men can ever know; have transcended the sense-world in order to live on high levels, the spiritual life."[1]

---

[1] Evelyn Underhill, *Mysticism* (New York: E.P. Dutton, Inc., 1961), pp. 34-35.

THE WORLD
OF THE MYSTIC

Chapter One

Who Is a Mystic and What Is Mysticism?

Mysticism is the belief in
a Reality beyond reality.
S.U.

Who Is a Mystic?

here are two different types of individuals in relation to their interest in the material and the spiritual world. There is, on the one hand, the person who has little or no interest in the world beyond the senses. He responds to the world which his senses report to him and to a large measure limits himself to that world. He lives biologically and seems to care little about intrinsic values, and is hardly

23

conscious, if at all, of transcendent Realities. This type
of man, however, is not completely devoid of spiritual
capacity and entirely composed of materiality. His
unconcern is due more to the influences of nurture and
social pressures than to an original bent of mind. This
man, as much as he may be unconcerned with the
spiritual aspects of life, may some day be shaken and
awakened to its reality and its importance to his being.

The other type of man is one who is saturated with
the world of the Spirit. He is not satisfied with mere
biological existence. He possesses a peculiar gift of
sensitivity for the deeper environment of the soul. He is
conscious of a Reality beyond reality. He is a representative of those individuals who are considered the spiritual adventurers of the human race. He is a mystic.

A mystic, then, may be said to be one who is consumed by a belief that the world which he experiences
through his senses is a mere veil which hides from him
the Real World. Penetrating this veil, by which he feels
separated from true Reality, is his paramount concern
and highest objective.

But what is it that leads the mystic to the belief that
there is something beyond; something more, than what
his senses report to him of the familiar world? The
mystic is convinced that in addition to his senses man
possesses an inner light, a level of consciousness by
which he can transcend materiality and thereby make
contact with the Soul of the universe—or, as Ralph
Waldo Emerson termed it, the "Over Soul."

Stated in another way, the mystic believes in the
possibility of direct intercourse with the Being of
beings, not through revelations, rituals, prayers, or
other such media. God, to the mystic, ceases to be an
object and becomes an experience.

The mystic lives at different levels of experience,

levels of consciousness, and this means that he sees a different world from the non-mystic; since the world as the non-mystic knows it is the product of certain scraps or aspects of reality acting upon a normal, untransfigured consciousness.

As other men are immersed in and react to natural or intellectual life, so the mystic is immersed in and reacts to the spiritual life. He moves toward a complete identification, complete "union with God."

The mystic in a way may be compared with the earthly artist. For as the artist tries to give us in color, sound, or words a hint of his ecstasy, a glimpse of truth, and finds how little of it he can convey, so the mystic tries but fails in his attempt to tell the world his secret.

"Of all the arts,. . . music alone shares with great mystical literature the power of waking in us a response to the life-movement of the universe; brings us, we know not how, news of its exultant passions and incomparable peace."[2]

What is Mysticism?

From what we know of mystics, we can say that mysticism is the immediate consciousness of God, the direct experience of religious truth.

"Mysticism," says Rufus Jones, "is an immediate, intuitive knowledge of God. . . or of transcendent Reality or of Divine Presence."[3]

In the words of Evelyn Underhill, "Mysticism is not an opinion; it is not a philosophy. It has nothing in common with the pursuit of occult knowledge. On the

---

[2] Underhill, *Mysticism*, p. 76.
[3] Rufus M. Jones, *The Flowering of Mysticism* (New York: Hafner Publishing Co., 1971), p. 25.

one hand, it is not merely the power of contemplating
Eternity; on the other, it is not to be identified with any
religious queerness. It is the name of that organic process which involves the perfect consummation of the
Love of God; the achievement here and now of the
immortal heritage of man, or, if you like it better, for
this means the same thing—it is the art of establishing
his conscious relation with the Absolute."[4]

Mysticism, according to Edward Caird, is "religion
in its most concentrated and exclusive form, as that
attitude of mind in which all other relations are swallowed up in the relation of the Soul to God."[5]

The Emergence of Mysticism

Mysticism is a response to man's deep desire to experience a closeness with God—or, as the mystic would
say it, a oneness with the "Over Soul."

Now, at what point in the history of the human race
did mysticism arise to satisfy this strong spiritual
desire? During his primitive period of existence, man
had no need for mysticism. In this period his environment was full of gods. On his every turn he was surrounded by them. He was close to what he believed to be
God.

When man advanced intellectually, morally, and
spiritually, his concept of God changed accordingly. At
this time God was viewed by him as a transcendent
being; but one who allows himself to be reached by
obeying certain laws, by establishing places and times
for worshiping him, and performing various rituals in

---

[4]   Underhill, *Mysticism*, p. 81.

[5]   Edward Caird, *The Evolution of Theology in the Greek Philosophers*, 3 vols. (Glasgow, 1904), ii, p. 210.

his honor. This approach to God occasioned institutional religion.

In the early stage of institutional religion, man's need for feeling close to the Absolute, or God, was fully satisfied. With the passing of time, however, institutional religion involved itself more and more with the material world; its mission consequently lost its pristine fire and fervor. The more sensitive individuals no longer felt that institutionalized religion was satisfying them. They began, therefore, to seek satisfaction for their spiritual need elsewhere. It was at this juncture that mysticism emerged and spread wherever man was in search of a formula for closing the gulf between himself and God.

Source of the Mystical Faculty

Mysticism views the essence of life and the world as an all-embracing spiritual substance and the human personality as a duality. One aspect of human nature, mysticism asserts, is the result of its relation with the material objects of the universe contacted by the senses. The other aspect of human nature is derived from its participation in the universal spiritual substance of life. Now, as man's bodily senses keep him informed of the world of matter, so that higher aspect of his nature, which acts as intermediary between the Supreme Universal Reality and his circumscribed person, is endowed with the faculty which makes him aware of the modalities of the transcendent realm to which it pertains. This is held to be the source of the mystical faculty.

Each aspect of man's nature is directed toward the particular area whence it derives its being and thrives in proportion to the amount of attention and interest it receives from the individual. Thus, the mystic finds it necessary to subdue his earthly concerns, desires, and appetites, in order to enable his spiritual faculties to develop to the point of becoming conscious of belonging to or of entering the realm of spiritual Unity.

The Mystical Experience

Mystical experience is marked by the emergence of a type of consciousness which is not sharply or clearly differentiated into a subject-object state. The "subject" and "object" are fused into an individual one. Whatever is seen, heard, or felt in these moments is flooded with an inrush from the abysses of the inner life. Deeplying powers, not ordinarily put into play, seem suddenly liberated. The usual insulations, which sunder our inner life into something like compartments, seem shot through. The whole being—in an integral and undivided experience—finds itself. Not only so, but transcendent energies from beyond the margin appear to "invade" the individual self; a larger, environing consciousness, an enfolding presence, makes itself felt.

The undifferentiated experiences, termed by some as "transcendental consciousness" occur in a variety of fields, in numerous ways, and with different degrees of depth and inclusiveness. Lofty appreciation of beauty or sublimity, absorbed enjoyment of music, serene companionship with nature, sudden insight into the meaning of a truth, the awakening of love, moral exultation of life in the pursuit of duty—all are examples of experiences which immensely transcend "knowledge" experiences, in which "subject" and "object" are fused into an undifferentiated one, and in which self is identified with object.

Religious mystical experience is an intense and strikingly dynamic variety of this fused, undifferentiated consciousness. The individual soul feels vitalized, merged with enfolding presence, liberated and exalted with a sense of having found what it has always sought.

The mystical experience, especially in the loftiest spiritual geniuses, may very well be the emergence of a new type-level of life, a higher manner of correspondence with ultimate sources of reality, a surge of the entire self towards ineffable fullness of life. It may be, in the higher sphere of the inner life, an instance of what biologists call a tropism—an inherent tendency of a living thing to turn towards the sources of its nutriment.

The mystical experience itself, as an inner life event, is unmistakably one of the great taproots of personal religion, bringing, as it does, to the recipient undemonstrable, but at the same time irrefragable, certainty of higher personal life in contact with the personal self, and revealing a superaddition of life-functions and new depth-levels of truth.

Stages toward the Mystical Experience

There seems to prevail a general method employed by mystics of all races and all faiths by which they are led from the experience of the sensory world of separate objects to a new world of unity in which the mystical experience is realized. This method consists of three different stages leading to the final experience.

First, there is the purgative stage—which involves the preliminary elimination of worldly interests and the eradication of the passions originating from them.

The second stage leading toward the mystical experience is attained when the soul has succeeded in detaching itself from the coarse appetites and the allurements of materiality, thus reaching a degree of increased enlightenment and inner freedom.

The third stage leading toward the mystical experience is achieved when the battle against earthly nature is won and the union between the mystic and the divine object of his quest takes place.

The Mystic Way

Mysticism is completely an activity of the spirit. "The spirit of the mystic," says Johannes Tauler, "is, as it were, sunk and lost in the Abyss of the Deity, and loses the consciousness of all creature distinctions. All things are gathered together in one with the divine sweetness, and the man's being is so penetrated with the divine substance that he loses himself therein, as a drop of water is lost in a cask of strong wine. And thus the man's spirit is so sunk in God in divine union that he loses all sense of distinction. . . and there remains a secret, still union, without a cloud of color."[6]

Spiritual desires are useless, the mystics claim, unless the whole self is properly conditioned and directed toward the Real. The Mystic Way is a trying psychological and spiritual process which entails "the remaking of character and the liberation of a new, or rather latent, form of consciousness which imposes on the self the condition which is sometimes called 'ecstasy' but is better named the Unitive State."[7]

[6]   Johannes Tauler, *Sermon for Septuagesima Sunday*, trans. Susanna Winkworth (London, 1906), p. 253.
[7]   Underhill, *Mysticism*, p. 81.

The Distinctive Mark of the Mystic

The mystic's most distinctive mark is love. His love is expressed in a deep-seated desire of his soul toward its Source. God, say the mystics, cannot be known by reason, but only by the love of one's heart. The mystic seeks to surrender himself to ultimate Reality, not for any personal gain or worldly joys, but purely from an instance of love. The mystic is in love with the Absolute.

Mystical States of Mind

After a mystical experience, the mystic finds it impossible to report to others the feelings of his experience. It is a state of mind which must be experienced directly. As Tennyson writes:

Moreover, something is or seems
That touches me with mystic gleams,
Like glimpses of forgotten dreams.

Of something felt, like something here;
Of something done, I know not where,
Such as no language may declare.[8]

In addition to experiencing a state of feeling, the mystic also experiences a state of insight. In his moment of trance he is afforded depths of truth unplumbed by the discursive intellect. He experiences illuminations and revelations which, like his feelings, he cannot share with others.

Mystical states of feeling or insight, mystics report,

---

[8] Alfred Tennyson, *The Two Voices.*

cannot be sustained for long. Only in rare instances do they last for more than two hours.

Mystical states are generally involuntary but they may be facilitated by certain voluntary exercises with both the mind and the body; and when this characteristic sort of consciousness sets in, the mystic feels as if his own will were in abeyance, and as if he were seized and held by a superior power.

The mystic considers whatever knowledge he experienced during his mystical state as valid for him as any knowledge acquired by someone in a non-mystical state.

Now, if mystics cannot communicate their experiences, how do we know anything about them at all? The answer is that although the mystic fails to convey to others his complete and full experience, yet there is something of it that remains in his memory of which he can speak and from which we can gain an inkling of his unusual state of mind.

What One Remembers after a Mystical Experience

Here is an example of what one mystic remembers of his mystical experience. The report is from the German idealist, Malwida von Meysenbug:

> I was alone upon the seashore as all these thoughts flowed over me, liberating and reconciling; and now again, as once before in distant days in the Alps of Dauphiné, I was impelled to kneel down, this time before the illimitable ocean, symbol of the Infinite. I felt that I prayed as I had never prayed before, and knew now what prayer really is: to return from the solitude of individuation into the consciousness of unity with all that is, to kneel down as one that passes away, and to rise up as one imperishable. Earth, heaven, and sea

resounded as in one vast world-encircling harmony. It was as if the chorus of all the great who had ever lived were about me. I felt myself one with them, and it appeared as if I heard their greeting: "Thou too belongest to the company of those who overcome."[9]

Here is another example of a mystical experience drawn from the memory of J. Trevor, who recorded it in his autobiography:

One brilliant Sunday morning, my wife and boys went to the Unitarian Chapel in Macclesfield. I felt it impossible to accompany them—as though to leave the sunshine on the hills, and go down there to the chapel, would be for the time an act of spiritual suicide. And I felt such need for new inspiration and expansion in my life. So, very reluctantly and sadly, I left my wife and boys to go down into the town, while I went further up into the hills with my stick and my dog. In the loveliness of the morning, and the beauty of the hills and valleys, I soon lost my sense of sadness and regret. For nearly an hour I walked along the road to the "Cat and Fiddle," and then returned. On the way back, suddenly, without warning, I felt that I was in Heaven—an inward state of peace and joy and assurance indescribably intense, accompanied with a sense of being bathed in a warm glow of light, as though the external condition had brought about the internal effect—a feeling of having passed beyond the body, though the scene around me stood out more clearly and as if nearer to me than before, by reason of the illumination in the midst of which I seemed to be placed. This deep emotion lasted, though with decreasing strength, until I reached home, and for some time after, only gradually passing away.[10]

---

[9]   William James, *Varieties of Religious Experience* (New York: The Modern Library), pp. 386-7.
[10]   Ibid, p. 388.

Beliefs of Mysticism

Mysticism is characterized by certain beliefs. One belief of mysticism is that there is a kind of wisdom that is sudden, penetrating, and independent of the senses.

A second belief of mysticism is that there is a unity. It rejects the idea of division anywhere.

A third belief of mysticism is that time is unreal. This belief flows from its belief of unity and its rejection of division. If all is one, then the idea of past and future is unreal.

Mysticism and Individuality

Individuality according to mysticism implies separateness; it therefore contradicts mysticism's chief doctrine of oneness.

Mysticism denies divisibility in the universe; it nullifies that separateness of "I, Me, and Mine." In its essentiality mysticism seeks to transcend the limitations of the individual standpoint and surrender itself to ultimate Reality.

As mysticism disregards individuality, so it also transcends the barriers which separate race from race and religion from religion. To the mystic, the differences between the demands, beliefs, and observances of one creed and another are entirely obliterated in his all-absorbing and all-overshadowing passion for union with what he refers to as the All.

Mysticism and Intuition

Mysticism, like philosophy, arises from the elemental human desire to search and investigate both natural and spiritual phenomena and to understand their manifestations more thoroughly. But, while philosophy relies mainly on human reason and accepts it as the standard, mysticism—permeated with the emotional, religious feeling inherent in man—is, in addition to reason, actuated by intuition, a concept through which mystics believe direct and immediate truth is achieved.

Henri Bergson (1869-1949) protests against the excessive tribute paid to the intellect, or intelligence, and to science as the ripest fruit of intelligence. Intelligence, according to Bergson, has for its original function the construction and use of inorganic tools in the service of life. It is, therefore, most at home in the world of inert solids. Now, for the practical purpose of making tools, it is convenient to treat material bodies as discrete units each *divisible ad libitum*. But when intelligence becomes theoretical, and seeks to explain life and thought as well as inert matter, then it leads astray. For it tends to treat all things as if they consisted of lifeless matter, and the whole of reality is reduced to a dead mechanism, for intelligence is unable to comprehend life.

This defect of intelligence must be made good by intuition, for it can reveal the most intimate secrets of life. Intuition, according to Bergson, leads us to the very inwardness of life as successfully as intelligence guides us into the secrets of matter. Human consciousness is predominantly intellectual. But man is not entirely lacking in intuition, which functions whenever our deepest interests are at stake.[11]

---

[11]   See Henri Bergson, *Introduction to Metaphysics.*

Rational and Spiritual Consciousness

Our normal or rational consciousness is our awareness of the sense world in which we operate on a daily
basis. This form of consciousness is vital to our survi-
val; it warns us of danger to our physical being; it
points to the tools that we are to employ in coping with
our material problems.

In addition to the normal or rational form of consciousness, there is another that man possesses. This
form may be called the spiritual consciousness.

Some people may go through life without suspecting
that they possess it. Those who know of its presence
within themselves are stimulated by it, experience life
on a higher plane. Those people are poets, novelists,
playwrights, composers, musicians, and painters.

A few individuals are so inspired by their spiritual
form of consciousness that for a moment they are lifted
out of the world of matter and enter a world which
appears to them more beautiful, more real than the
phenomenal world. These few are the mystics.

How the Mystic Differs from the Ordinary Religionist

The mystic differs from the ordinary religionist in
that, whereas the latter knows God through an objective revelation whether in nature or as embodied in the
Bible (which is really only secondhand knowledge,
mediate, external, the record of other people's vision
and experiences), the mystic knows God by contact of
spirit with spirit. He has the immediate vision; he
hears the "still, small voice" speaking clearly to him in
the silence of his soul. In this sense the mystic stands
quite outside the field of all the great religions of the

world. Religion to him is merely his own individual religion, his own lonely, isolated quest for truth. He is solitary, a soul alone with God.

Upon examining the lives and works of mystics, however, we usually find that, in spite of their intensely individualistic type of religion, they are related to one particular religion of the world. Their mystical experiences are colored and molded by one dominant faith. The specific forms of their conceptions of God do not come from their own inner light only, but from the teachings which they absorb from the external and traditional religion of their race or country. Thus, we find Jewish Mysticism, Christian Mysticism, Islamic Mysticism, Buddhist Mysticism, and Hindu Mysticism. The goal that each type stresses, however, is the same for all mystics.

The Difference between Mysticism and Organized Religion

Mysticism, the religion of the mystic, is religion in its purest form. Unlike the "Organized" type of religion, it is free of intermediaries, established prayers, set times and places for worship, special observances, and a host of other requirements.

In actuality, all the practices, all the accoutrements that are associated with the conventional type of religion, are not religion in the true sense. They are intended as a means by which the religious spirit of an individual is to be awakened and helped to rise to a higher, more sensitive level of spiritual consciousness, to transcend the sense world.

More often than not the practitioner of the "Organized" type of religion mistakes the form of his religion for its substance. Few, very few, therefore experience, as the mystic does, a direct relationship with the Absolute.

Even though institutionalized religion may not satisfy the spiritual need of the mystic, yet, he does not oppose it. He knows that it fills a need for his brother man, a need which in the eyes of the mystic is really more social than religious.

Two Theories of Divine Reality

Two theories of Divine Reality that have been propounded by theologians and accepted by mystics are known by the names of Emanation and Immanence.

The Emanation theory maintains that all existing things in the universe are outflowings of God. Everything in the cosmos, all finite creatures animate as well as inanimate, radiate in a successive series from God, the Perfect One.

This theory attempts to explain the difficulties involved in the inevitable assumptions of all religion: that there is a bond of relationship between God and His creation. "How can there be," it is asked, "any connecting link between a Being who is self-sufficient, changeless, infinite, and perfect, and matter which is finite, changeable, and imperfect?" This is the question. All doctrines of emanation answer the question by saying that God is not really external to anyone or anything. The multiplicity that one beholds in the cosmos, the forms and essences which make up the visible universe, are all an unfolding of the divine, all emanations from the Spirit. God is at one and the same time both the matter and form of the universe. But He is also something more. He is not identical with the universe. He is greater than it; He transcends it.

To those who identify with the Immanence theory, the quest of the Absolute results in a realization of something which is implicit in the self and in the universe: an opening of the eyes of the soul upon the Reality in which it is immersed. For them the earth is literally "crammed with heaven." The Absolute does not hold Himself aloof from an imperfect, material universe, but dwells within the flux of things. "God," says Plotinus, "is with all things."[12] He is not far from any of us, for in Him we live and move and have our being.

According to the Immanence doctrine, the world is not projected from the Absolute but immersed in Him; the universe is free, self creative. The divine action floods it. No part is more removed from the Godhead than any other part. The divine spark is latent alike in the cosmos and in man.

Mysticism and Freedom

The mystic, of all the people in the world, enjoys genuine and complete freedom. The freedom of the mystic is derived from his inner being. He achieves it by detaching himself from things material, external, and by avoiding those things which promise much but in the end offer nothing but emptiness, disillusionment, and disappointment.

The mystic knows that man's desire for things never ends. He forever remains hungry. No matter how much he has, he wants more and more. And in his drive to gain more, newer, and better things, he is always in a state of restlessness and disturbance. His goal is never met, it continuously recedes; his pursuit after it ends only when his life does. No one has ever declared that

---

12   Plotinus, *Ennead*, vi, p. 9.

he has attained serenity of spirit, inner freedom, as a result of his material treasures.

"In detachment," says St. John of the Cross, "the spirit finds quiet and repose for coveting nothing... for as soon as it covets anything, it is immediately fatigued thereby."[13]

Once an individual succeeds in transcending his cravings for materiality, that which promises and does not fulfill, that which allures and ultimately ensnares and enslaves, the downward drag is at an end. "Then a free spirit in a free world, the self moves upon its true orbit, undistracted by the largely self-imposed needs and demands of ordinary earthly existence."[14] This free spirit, which may be termed as the redeemed self, is that of the mystic. He alone knows the meaning of inner peace and freedom in its deepest sense.

How the Non-Mystic Views the Mystic

In his famous Allegory of the Cave, Plato presents two aspects of reality. He describes a race of people which for several centuries was confined to a cave. In this cave, they could see nothing but the shadows of images projected against the wall as they passed along a ledge between the wall and a fire. Reality to them consisted of the shadows, for that was all they had been accustomed to seeing.

One day a young man received permission to leave the cave. As he approached its mouth he was repulsed by the bright light of the sun. He waited until evening and then went forth into the outside world. He found that even the light of the moon and stars was too strong

---

[13] St. John of the Cross, *The Ascent of Mt. Carmel*, trans. D. Lewis (London, 1906), Bk. I, Chap. xiii.
[14] Underhill, *Mysticism*, p. 207.

for his weakened eyes. After some time, when his vision improved, he began to notice the beauty and splendor that surrounded him. For a while he could not believe that the world he was seeing was real, but he soon began to realize that, rather than the real world, it was the shadows of the cave that in fact were empty of meaning and reality. Wishing to share his incredible experience with his compatriots whom he had left behind, he therefore returned to the cave. By this time, he no longer possessed the capacity to tolerate the darkness or see any meaning in the shadows. When he began to relate to his fellow prisoners the wonders and magnificence of the outside world, they mocked him and considered him mad. The outside world, they concluded, had caused him to lose both his sight and his mind. They resolved that in the future any one of them who would attempt to leave the cave, forsake the security of the real world for the illusion of the outside world, would be severely punished.[15]

Plato's allegory indirectly portrays the attitude of the non-mystic toward the mystic. Like the young man of the cave who discovers true reality outside of it, the mystic discovers a reality independent of the senses. But when he reports his discovery to his fellowmen whose lives are grounded in the sense world, whose spirituality lies dormant in them, they listen to his tale of excitement with suspicion, and think of him as having lost his way.

What the Mystics Say to the Non-Mystics

"We come to you not as thinkers, but as doers. Leave your deep and absurd trust in the senses, with their language of dot and dash, which may possibly report fact but can never communicate personality. If phil-

---

[15]   Plato, *Republic* 7, 514a-521b.

osophy has taught you anything, she has surely taught you the length of her tether, and the impossibility of attaining to the doubtless admirable grazing land which lies beyond it. One after another, idealists have arisen who, straining frantically at the rope, have announced to the world their approaching liberty, only to be flung back at last into the little circle of sensation. But here we are, a small family, it is true, yet one that refuses to die out, assuring you that we have slipped the knot and are free of those grazing grounds. This is evidence which you are bound to bring into account before you can add up the sum total of possible knowledge, for you will find it impossible to prove that the world as seen by the mystics, 'unimaginable, formless, dark with excess of bright,' is less real than that which is expounded by the youngest and most promising demonstrator of a physico-chemical universe. We will be quite candid with you. Examine us as much as you like: our machinery, our veracity, our results. We cannot promise that you shall see what we have seen, for here each man must adventure for himself; but we defy you to stigmatize our experiences as impossible or invalid. Is your world of experience so well and logically founded that you dare make of it a standard? Philosophy tells you that it is founded on nothing better than the reports of your sensory apparatus and the traditional concepts of the race. Certainly it is imperfect, probably it is illusion; in any event, it never touches the foundation of things. Whereas 'what the world, which truly knows *nothing*, calls "mysticism," is the science of *ultimates*. . . the science of self-evident Reality, which cannot be "reasoned about," because it is the object of pure reason or perception.' "[16]

---

[16] Coventry Patmore, *The Rod, the Root, and the Flower*, 2nd ed. (London, 1907), "Aurea Dicta," cxxviii.

Chapter Two

Hindu Mysticism

Mysticism is looking at the Universe
with the eye of the soul.

S.U.

The Mystical Temper of the Indian People

here are no people who have been more powerfully and continually affected by the thought of a spiritual world than the people of India, and it is accordingly to be expected that among them the mystical temper of mind should be found. But, while the sense of the reality of the spiritual creates this temper among Hindus no less than among earnest souls elsewhere, we find that Hindu thought possesses

43

two characteristics which are closely related to each other and indeed complementary, and which at the same time belong to the very nature of mysticism. These are its doctrine of *maya*[17] and its monism. That preoccupation with the spiritual world which is the essence of mysticism inevitably involves a view that, at the least, lightly esteems the world of sense. In its contempt of the finite Hindu thought is in fullest accord with the mystic spirit in all its manifestations. So also, in its determined quest for an ultimate unity, Hinduism discovers itself at one with mysticism, since, as William James affirms, "mystical states of mind in every degree are shown by history, usually though not always, to make for the monistic view."[18]

In Hinduism, indeed in nearly all its manifestations in its most philosophical flights, there are to be found indications of the mystical temper of mind. One reason for this appears to lie, as far as it is possible to pierce the secret of the soul of a race, in the intense preoccupation of the Indian people from the earliest or at least from immediately post-Vedic times with the desire to escape from selfhood as the one way to ultimate peace. The passion of this pursuit was, perhaps, intensified by the accompanying belief, wherever it may have been obtained, in the power of *karma* and in the long travail of transmigration. The only deliverance from the endless revolution of the wheel of *samsara* was realized to lie in an escape to a region which, because there is no consciousness there, must necessarily be a barren and an empty land. Thus the quest of Hinduism is impelled onward by two allied impulses which at the same time strengthen and contradict each other. It is an escape and an attainment, but in the escape from the bondage

---

[17]   *Maya* refers to false conceptions about oneself and the world.
[18]   William James, *Pragmatism* (London, 1907), p. 151.

of the self the union with the ultimate One is emptied of all sense of realization and, in the words of Bahva to Vaskali, "That *Atman* is silence."[19] It is this contradiction that gives to so much of Indian thought that "troubled intensity" which Edward Caird finds also in the writings of Plotinus, justifying the claim for it, as for them, that it is among the highest expressions of the mystic spirit.[20]

The Vedic Age

The earliest knowledge we have of the Indian people and their ways, civilization, and religion is derived from the Rig-Veda. Veda means "knowledge," preeminently religious knowledge, and is applied in later times to the whole sacred literature regarded as revealed. The Rig-Veda is a collection of poems in ten books. Most of them are hymns of praise and prayer addressed to particular gods or groups of gods. Many of the hymns were composed by priestly poets for princely patrons to be recited or sung on sacrificial occasions. The poets sometimes ascribed the thoughts embodied in their verses to divine inspiration.

From the hymns we learn something of the character of the gods to whom they were dedicated, the things which they were desired and expected to do for their worshippers, the conditions of their favor, and the feelings with which men approached them.

The gods were in the main the great powers of nature which affect human welfare or the objects and phenomena in which these powers are manifested—the

---

[19] *Sankara on Brahmasutra*, iii, ii, 17.
[20] Edward Caird, *Greek Philosophers*, vol. 2, p. 233.

bright sky, the enlivening sun, the rosy dawn, the storm which brings the longed-for rain.

Of course, as in all such cases, it was not the natural object or phenomenon as such that was worshipped, but a power actuated by a will and prompted by motives such as determine human conduct, and conceived, after the analogies of primitive physiological psychology, as a spirit. Even when his name seemed to identify him with a natural object—as, for example, *Surya*, the sun—the god was thus in his inner nature like man, and the myths also gave him human form, and described solar phenomena as human doings.

The Brahmanas

The centuries following the age of the Vedic hymns may be described as the Brahmanic period. In it the great body of ritual works which are called Brahmanas was elaborated and attained fixed form in the tradition of the several Vedic schools.

The Brahmanas are primarily minute prescriptions for the performance of religious rites; but to these are attached explanations of the origin and significance of the ceremonies as a whole or of particular details in them. This commentary on the rites finds not infrequent occasion for theological or philosophical digressions the starting-point of which is usually the cosmogonic problem, the authorship of the universe.

The Creation of the World

The creation of the world is ascribed to Prajapati in a Rig-Veda hymn.[21] He brought it into existence out of

---
[21]   Rig-Veda x, 121.

himself. Prajapati was believed to have been not only the author of the universe, but its upholder and ruler as well.

Another cosmogonic hymn speaks of a time when there was neither being nor non-being.[22] It names no god, only "that One" besides which was naught else. A still different conception of the origin of the world, is set forth in the hymn of the *Purusha*.[23] Man, as the microcosm, has often been set over against the universe-macrocosm; here, on the contrary, the universe is imagined as the infinite man.

One can easily see how during this period poets and thinkers struggling to express theologically, or metaphysically, in accordance with their ability, the idea that at the origin of all things there is one ground of being—one god, some would say—and call him creator; to others it is the nameless One.

The Upanishads

The subject of the One, which dominated the interest of the Indian mind, is discussed at length in the Upanishads.

What are the Upanishads? The name Upanishad (literally "session") means secret or esoteric teaching, mystery. The Upanishads contain, along with profound philosophical ideas, mystical speculations and mysterious rites. The older Upanishads are in prose, and usually in the form of a dialogue in which one who possesses the higher knowledge explains to an inquirer the nature of this knowledge and the way to attain it.

Even though the Upanishads deal with philosophical questions, they are far from resembling a philo-

---

22 Rig-Veda x, 129.
23 Rig-Veda x, 90.

sophical system. They represent the teachings of different thinkers over a period of several centuries. They go straight to the ultimate problems of metaphysics—the nature of reality, the relation of appearance and reality and of the many to the one.

The thinkers came to these questions from the mythological cosmogonic speculations of their predecessors; their thinking, like that of the earliest Greek philosophers, is often half mythical; they express themselves in mythical or ritualistic terms. Without being conscious of it, the same teacher sets forth views that seem to us to be inconsistent or even irreconcilable.

The Idea of Brahman

The Upanishads find the ground of the universe, the one reality, in a principle which is called Brahman. Brahman, as conceived by the authors of the Upanishads, is not only the successor of the Vedic gods, the highest and holiest reality of religion, but a sacred power, the source from which all things spring, the tie that holds all things together, and the That that all things are.

Brahman is not only the power but also the very essence of the Vedic gods. When asked how many gods there are, the sage Yajnavalkya reduced the traditional number to thirty-three, and finally to Brahman, one and one alone.[24]

Brahman, the one reality, is also called the Atman. The word denotes the "self," sometimes in an empirical sense the individual man; then, in a higher sense, his true self, in distinction not only from the body but from the inner organs of sense and cognition, which also are non-ego—in a word, the ideal self, the essential being.

---

[24]   Brihadaranyaka Upanishad 3. 9. 1-10.

In this higher sense the word is used of the Brahman, which is the ideal principle of the universe.

Atman and Brahman

The great mystery of the Upanishads is that the Atman in man is identical with the Atman in the universe—the Brahman. The soul of man is not a particle, an emanation, of the universal principle, but *is* that principle, whole and single. This idea is expressed truly in the Chandogya Upanishad:

> Verily the universe is Brahman. Let him whose soul is at peace worship it, as that which he fain would know.
>
> Of knowledge, verily, is a man constituted. As is his knowledge in this world, so when he hath gone hence, doth he become. After knowledge, then, let him strive.
>
> Whose substance is spirit, whose body is life, whose form is light, whose purpose is truth, whose essence is infinity—the all-working, all-wishing, all-smelling, all-tasting one that embraceth the universe, that is silent, untroubled.
>
> That is my spirit within my heart, smaller than a grain of rice or a barley-corn, or a grain of mustard-seed; smaller than a grain of millet, or even than a husked grain of millet.
>
> This my spirit within my heart is greater than the earth, greater than the sky, greater than the heavens, greater than all worlds.
>
> The all-working, all-wishing, all-smelling, all-tasting one that embraceth the universe, that is silent, untroubled—that is my spirit within my heart; that is Brahman. Thereunto, when I go hence, shall I attain. Who knoweth this; he, in sooth, hath no more doubts.
>
> Thus spake Candilya, Candilya.[25]

---

[25] Chandogya Upanishad iii, 14.

In other Upanishads the same idea, that Brahman and Atman are one and the same, is expressed thus:

> All this is Braham [neuter]. . . He [it] is myself within the heart. . . smaller than a mustard seed, smaller than a canary seed, or the kernel of a canary seed. He also is myself within the heart, greater than the earth, greater than the sky, greater than the heaven, greater than all these worlds.[26]

> Thou art woman, thou art man; thou art youth, thou art maiden; thou art an old man tottering along on thy staff; thou art born with thy face turned everywhere. Thou art the dark blue bee, thou art the green parrot with red eyes, thou art the thunder-cloud, the seasons, the seas. Thou art without beginning; thou art infinite, thou from whom all worlds are born.[27]

And yet at the same time He, the Self, is to be described by "No, no. He is incomprehensible, for he cannot be comprehended."[28]

The Brahman, the power which presents itself to us embodied in all beings, which brings into existence all worlds, supports and maintains them, and again reabsorbs them into itself, this external, infinite, divine power, is identical with the Atman, with what, after stripping off all that is external, we find in ourselves as our inmost and true being, our real self, the soul. From this identity of Brahman and Atman the pregnant formula is found in the "great word" *tat tvam asi*, "That art Thou."[29]

---

[26] Chandogya Upanishad iii, 14.
[27] Svetasvatara Upanishad iv, iii, 4.
[28] Bridhadaranyaka Upanishad iii, ix, 26; iv, iv, 22.
[29] Chandogya Upanishad, vi, 8, 7f.

The highest blessedness that man ever envisioned was an endless life hereafter in the company of the gods. For this form of blessedness the Upanishads substituted oneness with God in the fullest meaning of the word, not a union to be realized after death but a present and eternal reality.

In its purest form the "identity of Brahman-Atman" is consistent idealistic monism. But the innate realism of the human mind, the necessity of garbing abstract thought in figurative or traditional language, the difficulty of the cosmical problem from this standpoint, and the inheritance of earlier speculations upon it combine to give to the enunciation of the teaching in many passages either a theistic or a pantheistic turn.

There are passages in the Upanishads in which Brahman appears, not as an attributeless being, but as the source of all light, the life from which all beings spring, the principle of order in the universe, or as a personal god, the supreme Lord. Brahman is the creator of the world—its material as well as its efficient cause, the ruler of the world—and the lot of the soul in the round of its rebirth is appointed by him in accordance with the deeds of a former life.

This lower knowledge of Brahman, according to Sankara, a ninth-century Indian philosopher, has its rewards.[30] The soul that has attained it takes at death the way of the gods to heavenly bliss, and progresses by stages toward true knowledge and final deliverance; it is vastly better off than those who, with no knowledge of Brahman at all, seek their good by the way of works, sacrifices, and observances and fare when life is over by the "way of the fathers" to the reward of their offerings in the moon; while those who have neither

[30] A summary of Sankara's philosophy on Brahman is given by Paul Deussen in his *Outline of the Vedanta Philosophy*, translated by J.H. Woods and C.B. Runke, 1906.

knowledge nor good works atone for their misdeeds in hell, thence to return to earth as beasts or as men of castes reckoned lower than beasts.

The lower theological knowledge cannot, however, bring salvation; for at bottom it is not knowledge but ignorance which ascribes attributes and personality to Brahman, and sets him, as creator and ruler, over against a world of finite reality, and above all, conceives him as another and a stranger to the soul itself.

The Doctrine of Transmigration of Souls

The doctrine of transmigration of souls is discussed in the Upanishads and eventually became an important aspect of the religion in India. Belief in the re-embodiment of human souls in human beings or animals is widespread among savages, and was doubtless nothing new in India. What is new in the Upanishads is that man's character and lot in this life are determined by his deeds in a former existence, and that what he now does in like manner determines what he shall be in a future existence.

The doctrine of the transmigration of souls is harmonized with the older belief in heaven and hell by making heaven and hell only temporary states of retribution between successive embodiments of the soul; this combination is found in the Upanishads in the lesson of the Five Fires.[31]

The prevalence of this belief in an endless series of lives upon each one of which man entered laden with the deeds of his previous life gave to the problem of salvation in India a new meaning and a new urgency.

---

[31] Bridhadaranyaka Upanishad, vi., 2; Chandogya Upanishad, v. 3, 10.

How can man escape this eternally revolving wheel of
birth and death?

The Upanishads have provided the secret of salvation in the oneness of Brahman-Atman. For him who
has attained this knowledge the illusion of separate
individuality is dissolved with all its consequences. He
is free from all desire—what can he wish who is all?—
his former deeds are consumed like rushes in the fire;
deeds done after the achievement of knowledge adhere
to him no more than water to the lotus-leaf.

He who is without desire, free from desire, his desire
attained, whose desire is set on Self [Atman], his vital
breath does not pass out, but Brahman is he, and in
Brahman is he absorbed. As the verse says:

> When all the passion is at rest
>   That lurks within the heart of man,
> Then is the mortal no more mortal,
>   But here and now attaineth Brahman.

> As a serpent's skin dead and cast off lies on an ant-hill,
> so lies this body then; but the bodiless, the immortal,
> the life is pure Brahman, is pure light.[32]

The attainment of union with the Brahman or the
severance of the true self from all that is not self was
sought, not alone by profound reflection, crowned in a
supreme moment by intuitive certainty, but by the use
of various means believed to conduce to the desired end
or to produce states favorable to its achievement.
Among these means ascetic self-mortification has a
large place. It is a common belief that privations and
inflictions which produce abnormal psychical states
bring supernatural knowledge and supernatural pow-

---

[32] Bridhadaranyaka Upanishad, iv, 4, 6.

ers; they have been employed in many higher religions for the attainment of an ecstatic experience the character of which is predetermined by expectation. Asceticism has had another significance where pessimistic conceptions of life have obtained. If existence is itself an evil, then the extinction of desire, which is the bond of attachment to existence, is the logical remedy. This is peculiarly true where desire is believed to be the cause of rebirth, or where desire as the motive of action is the ultimate cause of the burden of deeds which man carries from one life to another.

Other methods of inducing trance states are the practicing of certain exercises known as Yoga.

The chief purpose of the practice of Yoga is the use of the mind to suppress its own conscious movements, the whole body being so disciplined as to aid in the gradual suspension of consciousness and the bringing on of a state of pure ecstasy that is without thought and without sensation. The result is felt to be a complete freeing of the true self from the external world and natural causation.

The Word *Yoga*

The word *Yoga* comes from the same root as the English word "yoke"—and it means to bring together or unite. Yoga actually is a method of training designed to help man in the linking of his soul with the Godhead, or the Supreme Soul.

Types of Yoga

Of the various forms of Yoga that are prevalent in India, four are most commonly used. These are:

1. Jnana Yoga
2. Bhakti Yoga
3. Karma Yoga
4. Raja Yoga

The Aim of Yoga

The aim of each Yoga is the same. Why then are four different ones recommended? According to Hindu philosophers, there are four types of individuals. One type is basically reflective, a second one primarily emotional, a third one essentially active, and a fourth one characterized as empirical or experimental. For each of these types of individuals a particular Yoga is recommended and designed for the development of the endowments at his disposal. However, since no man is solely reflective, emotional, active, or experimental, Hinduism encourages individuals to test all four and combine them as best suits their predilections.

Jnana Yoga

Jnana Yoga is intended for spiritual aspirants who have a strong intellectual bent. The purpose of this Yoga, or method, is to enable one to attain undying bliss and a cessation of misery through the perception of the illusoriness of names and forms and the realization of the sole reality of Brahman which is identical with the human soul. The follower of this path must possess a keen power of reasoning by which he can distinguish the unreal from the real, the changing from the changeless. He must also develop indomitable will power to detach himself from the real and the changing. He cultivates such disciplines as have sway over

the mind and the senses, and which lead to inner calmness, forebearance, faith, and concentration. Above
all, he must have an intense longing for freedom
through the knowledge of truth.

Such an aspirant betakes himself to a qualified
teacher and is instructed about the identity of the soul
and Brahman. He reasons about this instruction and
then contemplates its meaning. Through uninterrupted
contemplation for a long time he at last attains an
exalted state of superconsciousness in which he realizes
oneness with Brahman.

Bhakti Yoga

For the emotional type, Hinduism prescribes Bhakti
Yoga, the path of divine love. The aspirant on this path
is called a devotee or lover of God. The devotee estab-
lishes with God a human relationship, regarding Him
as his Father, Master, Friend, or Beloved, according to
his prevailing mood. Divine love, unlike human affec-
tion, is free from fear, desire for reward, or any other
ulterior motive. A true devotee does not worship God
because he is afraid of punishment after death, or
because he expects happiness on earth or in heaven.

Because the loving principle in man is directed
toward unworthy, self-seeking purposes, the divine
harmony and felicity latent in man's heart is de-
stroyed. By abandoning all narrow and self-centered
affections, man allows the divine love to assert itself
pure and unalloyed in his interior universe.

Formal and ritualistic devotion, practiced for a long
time with sincerity and earnestness, is gradually
transformed into spontaneous and ecstatic love, which
destroys all the impurities of the devotee's heart and

reveals to him the ultimate oneness of love, lover, and beloved. In other words, the devotee realizes the aim of his quest, which is reaching unity with the "Over Soul" or Brahman.

Karma Yoga

For the active type, Hinduism prescribes Karma Yoga, or the method of right activity. The aspirant must perform every action regarding himself as God's instrument. He must surrender to God all the fruits of his actions, whether philanthropic, ritualistic, or those he performs every day for the maintenance of his body. A true Karma yogi serves others, seeing in them a manifestation of God. He regards with holy indifference success and failure and the good and bad results of his action. He cultivates a spirit of detachment from all worldly objects. To him every work is a form of worship and therefore sacred. He maintains an inner calmness being aware of his indissoluble relationship with God. Through the performance of action in the spirit of Yoga, the aspirant purifies his mind and ultimately attains the knowledge of God and union with Him.

Raja Yoga

Raja Yoga is intended for an individual of scientific bent. It is based on the idea of the soul being pure consciousness. Through right knowledge, Raja Yoga helps the soul realize its isolation from matter and attain freedom and perfection.
Raja Yoga prescribes the practical principles by

which the soul can detach itself from matter and realize its freedom. The Raja Yoga discipline consists of eight steps. The first two deal mainly with ethical principles, such as non-injury, truthfulness, continence, contentment, study of Scripture, and devotion to God. The third and fourth describe postures and breathing which are supposed to help in the practice of concentration and meditation, given in the remaining steps.

Through the practice of ethical disciplines the aspirant gradually weakens his violent desires, which disturb the surface of his mind. It is his mental agitation that prevents an individual from experiencing his inmost self. Through concentration, the aspirant strengthens his mind and cultivates inwardness of spirit. Through the one-pointed mind he practices contemplation, analyzes the different layers of consciousness, and at last realizes the true nature of his soul and its freedom from matter. He then feels touched by the higher spheres of the life of the world and begins to commune, as it were, with the deepest mysteries of the universe. He begins to feel part of the Infinite.

In every instance in the practice of Yoga, the aspirant's chief concern is to achieve unity with Brahman.

Chapter Three

Buddhism and Buddhist Mysticism

Mysticism is the religion of love.

S.U.

Introductory Note

ost systems of mysticism presented in this book are not preceded by a summary of the religion from which they stem. Buddhist mysticism, however, requires such a summary because it was first introduced as a religion without a belief in a god and a soul—two basics of religion generally and mysticism in particular.

Because these two basics were not included in primitive Buddhism, Buddhist mysticism was at first hardly possible or conceivable. Of course if Buddhism had remained in its original state then there could never be any Buddhist mysticism. For, as indicated in the opening chapter, mysticism is the soul's striving to unite with the Absolute or God.

But Buddhism did not remain in the form that was introduced by Buddha. After Buddha's death Buddhism split into numerous schools. Two of the largest and most popular of the schools are known by the names of Theravada and Mahayana.

The Theravadins adhered mostly to what they believed and understood to be the teachings of their master, Buddha.

The Mahayanists, on the other hand, interpreted Buddha's teachings more liberally, more broadly, and at the same time remained entrenched in the metaphysics of their mother religion—Hinduism. They reintroduced in their program of belief the two concepts which Buddha had not included, belief in a god and a soul.

Buddhist mysticism may be said, therefore, to be the product of the Mahayana school of Buddhism or Mahayanism. More about this school or branch of Buddhism will be given in the latter part of this chapter.

The Founder of Buddhism

The personal name of the founder of Buddhism was Siddhartha. His family name was Gautama, and Sakya was the name of the clan to which his family belonged. Siddhartha was born around the year 560

B.C. in Northern India approximately one hundred miles from Benares. He died about 480 B.C.

Siddhartha had every reason to be happy. His father was a king who lavished upon him every conceivable luxury. He was physically handsome and intellectually gifted. At the age of sixteen he married a neighboring princess by the name of Yosadhara. She was a model wife, charming, "full of dignity and grace." She bore him a beautiful son, whom they called Rahula.

Despite it all, sadness settled over him at the age of twenty. This eventually led him to completely break with his worldly estate.

The cause of Siddhartha's discontent is also the cause of the rise of Buddhism. Traditionally speaking, this is how it all began. When Siddhartha was born, his father asked astrologers to predict the future of his son. The astrologers prophesied that the boy was destined to become one of the greatest earthly rulers. But if he were to see four sights—disease, old age, death, and a monk who had renounced the world—then the boy would become the founder of a way of salvation for mankind.

Siddhartha's father, wishing that his son follow him as king, made every possible effort to keep him from the four sights and from all other unpleasant sights. He built a great palace in the midst of a park and ordered his servants not to allow the sick, the aged, a dead body, or a monk near the palace. The boy grew up shielded from any sight that would disturb him.

The gods, however, nullified the king's hopes and plans. On successive days, as Siddhartha was being driven through his park, he saw a man shaking with illness, a man tottering with age, a corpse being carried to its grave, and finally a monk in ochre robes who appeared peaceful and healthy. Siddhartha asked

what each of the sights meant and when he was told, he
was deeply saddened and began to meditate on the
meaning of life and upon man's destiny.

Siddhartha's Search for Enlightenment

One night there was a great feast with drunken
revelry in his palace. He alone remained awake and
sober. He surveyed the scene of debauchery and was
terribly disheartened by its apparent meaningless-
ness. It was that night that he resolved to renounce his
life of security, the life of self-indulgence, pleasure, and
material comfort. He went to the door of his bed-
chamber where his wife and son were asleep, bade
them both a silent goodbye, and left the palace, never to
return. He shaved off his hair, put on the robe of a
mendicant, and, like thousands of other ascetics in his
day, began to search for a way of salvation.

The first thing he did at this point was to put himself
under the guidance of two adepts in the art of cultivating trance states. But he was soon convinced that this
was not the way. He then turned to self-mortification.
His ascetic zeal attracted to him five other ascetics
expecting enlightenment from him. He pushed his fasting to such extremes that he brought himself to the
verge of death, and the result he was looking for eluded
him. This way having proved to be fruitless, he desisted
from such austerities. His companions lost faith in him
and left him, but Siddhartha seated himself under a
tree and vowed to stay there in meditation until he had
achieved enlightenment. At last, seven years after he
had begun his quest, as he was meditating beneath the
tree, the hour of illumination came. He experienced the
earthly foretaste of Nirvana, of ultimate salvation.

This experience of his is described as the moment of his becoming awake, *Bodhi*, becoming the enlightened one, the Buddha, to whom the founding of Buddhism is attributed.

After this exciting experience, Siddhartha faced the decision of keeping the experience to himself or sharing it with all others who might not understand it. He decided to share his experience with others.

First he sought out the five ascetics who had been the witnesses of his austerities and who had turned away from him when he had abandoned his extreme practices of deprivation. When the ascetics saw him approaching them with a radiant appearance, they arose and paid him homage. He spoke to them of his discovery, taught them the meaning of life, the way of salvation; then he and they went forth to spread the message of the Buddha. An order of monks, the *Sangha*, was founded and by the time of Buddha's death, forty-five years later, the new religion had thousands of adherents, among whom were included many members of Siddhartha's family.

Buddha's Basic Teachings

The discourse the Buddha held with the five ascetics, sometimes referred to as the Sermon at Benares, contains the fundamentals of the faith. The seeker of salvation should guard against the two extremes of self-indulgence and self-mortification; both are unprofitable. The true way is the middle way; following it, man arrives at peace of mind, knowledge, enlightenment, Nirvana. The middle way Buddha termed the Eightfold Path, which comprises right belief, right resolution, right speech, right conduct, right means of subsistence, right effort, right meditation, and right absorption. The Eightfold Path, according to the Buddha, is the remedy for man's miserable existence upon this earth.

The Four Noble Truths and the Eightfold Path

Man's miserable existence is succinctly summed up by Buddha in his Four Noble Truths.

The first of the Four Noble Truths states that life is suffering from the cradle to the grave. If there are a few moments during which the human being tastes a bit of happiness, these moments are of short duration.

The second of the Four Noble Truths asserts that there is a cause for human suffering and that the cause is rooted in human craving, the craving for things, for self-gratification and for the perpetuation of the self.

The third of the Four Noble Truths indicates that human craving may be cut and the individual freed from his or her misery.

But how can one eliminate cravings from his or her being? The way to this end, according to Buddha, is by following the Noble Eightfold Path.

Buddha's Conception of Salvation

Buddhism, like all the religions and religious philosophies which flourished during that period, is a way of salvation, and it has in common with them certain basic assumptions. Foremost among these is the belief that salvation must be achieved by each individual for himself. No god can deliver him. The Vedic gods, for example, have no powers or functions beyond the sphere of natural good; they are themselves subject to the cycle of rebirth, and themselves stand in need of salvation. Another point of agreement is the nature of the evil from which man is to be saved—the bondage to the ills of corporeal existence and the endless repetition of these ills in the infinite series of rebirths in which man enters every new existence burdened with the consequences of previous deeds. There is, however, one important difference between Buddha's conception of the problem of salvation and that of the other contemporary systems. They all assumed that there is a soul, an ego, which passes, with its load of deeds, from one existence to another to receive its just recompense of rewards; their starting point was the common notion of transmigration. Buddha, however, denied that there is any such thing corresponding to what common opinion or the technical speech of philosophers called soul.

Buddha held that the empirical individual is a transient combination of five components (*skandhas*); bodiliness, sensation, perception, predispositions, and consciousness. At death this complex is resolved into its elements. That there is no ego, no soul, is a fundamental tenet of primitive Buddhism.

Even though Buddha does not admit the transmigration of souls as it is commonly understood, for the reason that he does not believe in the existence of a permanent entity called soul which migrates, he nevertheless clings no less firmly to the belief in the round of rebirths and the dependence of each existence on preceding existences. A favorite illustration of his is that of one candle kindled from the flame of another; neither the second candle nor its flame is the same as the first, but without the former the latter would not be alight. Hence to the question; what passes from one life to another? The answer is karma and nothing but karma. This does not mean that the deed of one man is carried over to another; it is heresy to hold that he who experiences the fruit of a deed is different from the one who performed the deed, and it is equally heretical to assert that he is the same. Where the existence of a soul is denied, the question of identity has no meaning. But if a soul is denied, then how does a new existence depend upon a former one, and how is it determined by it? The formula of "dependent origination" is Buddhism's proposed solution to the problem. On (1) ignorance depends (2) the diathesis; on this, (3) (potential) intelligence and consciousness; on this, (4) individuation; on this, (5) the six spheres of sense (including the intellectual sense); on these, (6) contact (with their respective stimuli in the sensible and intelligible world); hence follow in order (7) feeling, (8) craving, (9) cleaving (to the world and life); then the new series: (10) beginning of existence (the formation of the embryo), (11) birth, (12) old age and death with all their train of sorrows—the so-called Twelve Causes. The formula has been diversely interpreted by Buddhists as well as by Occidental scholars. The point to bear in mind is that all that a man does in ignorance of the truth produces a certain complex of predispositions—we might say, a form of character with its accordant destiny—and this diathesis realizes itself in another life which is thus determined by that former life.

On Preventing Rebirth

While the theory of the chain by which one existence is linked to another may be obscure, there is no question that there is but one way to break its sequence; namely, to put an end to the production of karma. It is not action alone that does the mischief, the mere functioning of the physical and psychical mechanism, but the motivation, the craving for what people in their ignorance call the good things of this life, the blind clinging to life itself as a good, the desire for another life, the will to be. Cease all that and the deeds done without self-regarding motive or purpose have no consequence in them, their karma is barren. The karma left over from a former existence or accumulated in the present life before the attainment of this state must exhaust itself before the complete deliverance comes, as a potter's wheel keeps on revolving for a time by the force of the impulse given it but, if it receives no new impulse, gradually comes to rest, or as the lamp that is freshly fed with oil burns till the oil in it is consumed and then goes out. For such there is no rebirth.

For achieving this end, Buddha's Eightfold Path is to be followed. The first step in this path is right belief—that is, belief in the Four Noble Truths enunciated by Buddha; then follow right resolution, the resolve to renounce all sensual pleasures, to have malice toward none, and to harm no living creature; right speech, abstaining from backbiting, harsh language, falsehood, and frivolous talk; right conduct, not being guilty of unchastity; right means of subsistence, giving up a wrong occupation and getting one's livelihood in a proper way; right effort, the strenuous endeavor to overcome all faults and evil qualities, to attain, preserve, and cultivate all good qualities. These six paths are ways of moral self-discipline and might be comprehended under one head. The next, right reflection, might be called the intellectual discipline, a higher means by which man rids himself of lust and grief. The highest stage is the mystical discipline, right absorption, or concentration, a series of trances through

which an individual rises to the bliss which is as far
beyond happiness as beyond misery, reaches the intuition of higher and higher ranges of truth, and passes
into ecstasies that lie beyond consciousness.

The Arhat

The *arhat* ("saint") is the one in whom all causes of
moral imperfection are exhausted, all evil propensities
rejected. He has fulfilled his task, laid down his burden,
removed all bonds, obtained the four kinds of transcendent faculties; he is no longer subject to rebirth.

The Term *Nirvana*

The supreme goal of the arhat is Nirvana. The word
means literally "blowing out." For the Hindu, Nirvana
is a loss of individual identity by absorption of the
atman into the paramatman from whence it originated.

Buddhist Nirvana represents the waning of the
tanha, the cravings, desires, passions which tend to
perpetuate the cycle of rebirth. Without the fires of
craving, man is liberated from all attachments to the
world of matter.

This liberation while still in this world is an experience of inner peace. All that can be said with certainty about the early Buddhist conception of Nirvana
is that it meant a peaceful end unhaunted by the fear of
rebirth. This blessed assurance fills the saint with the
joy of salvation; the strife is over, the victory won.
Henceforth, what remains is perfect peace, endless
peace.

To attain the stage of sainthood is to follow scrupu-
lously the Eightfold Path.

The Arhat's Chief Quality and Buddha's Directive to Love Mankind

The chief quality of the arhat is benevolence. He is the Buddhist exemplar of what one may become, what one ought to be. Even though a Buddhist, if he literally follows the teachings of Buddha, is urged to concern himself with his own blessedness, to wander alone like a rhinoceros, nevertheless he is simultaneously charged to love all mankind. Buddha expressed love and compassion for all human beings, as is manifested in his teachings. Even though he strove to break every personal tie to special individuals based on emotion, because such ties are misery-producing, yet he commanded his disciples to love mankind with a mother's love.

> As a mother, even at the risk of her own life, protects and loves her child, so let a man cultivate love without measure toward all beings. Let him cultivate love without measure toward the whole world above, below, and around, unstinted, unmixed with any feeling of differing or opposing interests. Let a man remain steadfastly in this state of mind all the while he is awake, whether he be standing, walking, sitting, or lying down. This state of mind is the best in the world.[33]

Early Buddhist Ethics

Early Buddhist ethics are embodied in the Five Precepts, which are the foundation of the moral life for both the monastic and lay communities. Buddhists are to abstain from: destruction of life, taking what is not

---

[33] Metta Sutta, quoted from K. Morgan (ed.), *The Path of Buddha* (New York: The Ronald Press, 1950), p. 94.

given, unchastity, speaking falsely, and drinking "spirituous, strong, and maddening liquors."

Early Buddhist ethics followed a middle path between extreme asceticism on the one hand and extreme indulgence on the other.

In Hinduism one of the rewards for faithful observance of caste duties was rebirth in a higher caste. In the teachings of Buddha, stealing or adultery was regarded as the same reprehensible, immoral act regardless of the caste of the person committing the offense. People who kept the precepts were honored regardless of caste.

In two sutras of the *Majjhima Nikaya*, Buddha stated conclusively that morality, not birth, really counts; that being skilled in the *dharma* is the most important thing; and that men from any caste are capable of "taking a back-scratcher and bath powder and going to a river [and] capable of cleansing themselves of dust and mud."[34]

While Buddhists did not organize a movement against the caste system, they nevertheless ignored the caste restrictions, thus rendering them ineffective among the Buddhists.

Buddha and Speculation

Buddha was a rationalist. This means that he skirted metaphysics, avoided speculation about questions to which there are no conclusive answers. Any question or matter which the intellect could not deal with he steered clear from and warned his disciples also to avoid. He saw no value in raising questions concerning

---

[34]   *Majjhima Nikaya*, Vol. II, pp. 147-157; 177-181.

the presence of a heaven and hell, whether there is life after death, when the world began, and when, if ever, it will end. On matters of this sort, he spoke to his disciples in these words:

> Bear always in mind what it is that I have not elucidated, and what it is that I have elucidated. And what have I not elucidated? I have not elucidated that the world is eternal; I have not elucidated that the world is finite; I have not elucidated that the world is infinite; I have not elucidated that the soul and body are identical; I have not elucidated that the monk who has attained [the arhat] exists after death; I have not elucidated that the arhat does not exist after death; I have not elucidated that the arhat both exists and does not exist after death; I have not elucidated that the arhat neither exists nor does not exist after death. And why have I not elucidated this? Because this profit not, nor has to do with the fundamentals of religion, therefore I have not elucidated this.
>
> And what have I elucidated? Misery have I elucidated; the origin of misery have I elucidated; and the path leading to the cessation of misery have I elucidated. And why have I have elucidated this? Because this does profit, has to do with the fundamentals of religion, and tends to absence of passion, to knowledge, supreme wisdom, and Nirvana.[35]

The Primary Source for the Life and Teachings of Buddha

The primary source for the life and teachings of Buddha is an early body of Buddhist Scripture called the

[35]   Henry C. Warren, *Buddhism in Translation* (Cambridge: Harvard University Press, 1922), p. 122 (*Majjhima Nikaya 63*).

Tripitaka or The Three Baskets. The three divisions or baskets are:

The Vinaya Pitaka, the basket of disciplines, consisting of the rules of the Order;

The Sutta Pitaka, the basket of discourses, of the dialogues between Buddha and his disciples on his teachings of the religion; and

The Abhidhamma Pitaka, the collection of teachings on metaphysics.

The *Tripitaka* has been translated into English by the Pali Text Society of London.

The Final Days of Buddha

The last days and death of Buddha are described with great detail in a brief text called the *Book of the Great Decease*. Siddhartha was aware that death was near, suffering as he was from food poisoning, and he thus spoke to his close disciples who were with him:

> Be lamps unto yourselves. Be refuges to yourselves. Take yourselves to no external refuge. Hold fast to the Truth as a lamp. Hold fast as a refuge to the Truth.[36]

After an exchange in which no member of the Order who was in his presence on that day expressed any doubt about anything that he had ever taught them, he spoke to them in these words:

> Behold now, brethren, I exhort you, saying: "Decay is inherent in all component things! Work your salvation with diligence."[37]

---

[36] *The Dialogues of the Buddha (Digha Nikaya)*, trans. T.W. Rhys Davids (London: Oxford University Press, 1899-1921), Vol. II, p. 100.

[37] Ibid., pp. 155-156.

Buddhism after Buddha

After Buddha's death, disputes arose among his disciples as to the true meaning of certain of his doctrines. Since his teachings were not yet recorded in writing, there was little agreement on a number of questions pertaining to certain practices. The disputes among his disciples gave rise to two branches of Buddhism. One branch or division was called *Hinayana* (the small ferry) and the other took the name of *Mahayana* (the big ferry). The goal of each branch was to help man across the sea of sorrow to the shore of enlightenment and peace. But the way to the goal is what differentiated the two branches from each other.

The Hinayana branch of Buddhism, which eventually took the name of *Theravada* (The Way of the Elders), claimed to represent the teachings of the Buddha and the discipline he instituted. Buddhism, according to the Theravadins, was a full-time undertaking; it therefore did not expect everyone to make Nirvana his main goal, but those who did would have to relinquish the everyday world and become monks.

The second branch, the Mahayanists, maintained that Buddhism's outlook was as relevant for the layman as for the professional and that it applied to the work-a-day world as to the monastery. Of the two branches, the one which drew laymen to itself won the largest number of supporters. This branch claimed that its understanding of Buddhism was based not so much on Buddha's teachings but upon his life, which was in a way an interpretation of his teachings.

Other basic differences between the two branches of Buddhism are as follows:

1. Theravada Buddhism considers man as an in-

dividual whose emancipation from the suffering of life is completely in his own hands. He has no one to rely upon for his salvation except himself. Mahayana argues that the fate of each individual is linked with the fate of all.

2.   Theravada Buddhism centers on monks. Mahayana Buddhism is primarily a religion for laymen. Even its priests are expected to concern themselves with the welfare of laymen.

3.   The chief virtue in Theravada is *bodhi*, "wisdom." The key word in Mahayana is *karuna*, "compassion." Widsom without compassion in Mahayana's view is worthless.

4.   The ideal type of the Theravadins is the *arhat*, whose main objective is to attain Nirvana. In the Mahayanists the ideal type is the *bodhisattva*, a being who, having brought himself to the brink of Nirvana, voluntarily relinquishes his prize that he may return to the world to make it accessible to others. How the two ideal types differ from each other is graphically depicted in the story of four men who, journeying across an immense desert, come upon a compound surrounded with high walls. One of the four determines to find out what is inside. He scales the wall and on reaching the top gives a whoop of delight and jumps over. The second and third do likewise. When the fourth man gets to the top of the wall, he sees below him an enchanted garden with sparkling streams, pleasant groves, and tantalizing fruit. Though wishing to jump over, he resists the temptation. Remembering other wayfarers who are trudging through the

burning desert, he climbs back down and devotes himself to directing them to the oasis. The first three men were *arhats*; the last was a *bodhisattva*, one who vows not to forsake the world "until the grass itself be enlightened."

5. The two branches, Theravada and Mahayana Buddhism, also differ in their views of Buddha. To the Theravadins Buddha was a saint. For the Mahayanists Buddha was a savior. Among the Theravadins, Buddha was revered as a supreme sage, a man among men. When he entered Nirvana, his influence ceased. For the Mahavanists Buddha is a savior who continues to draw individuals toward him, who continues to exert influence on his followers forever.

A few other differences between the two divisions of Buddhism must be added to complete the picture. The Theravadins followed their leader by regarding speculation as a useless, pointless exercise, or as nothing more than a distraction. The Mahayanists developed an elaborate cosmology replete with innumerable heavens, hells, and descriptions of Nirvana. The only kind of prayer the Theravadins countenanced was meditation, whereas the Mahayanists added supplication, petition, and calling upon the name of the Buddha. Finally, whereas Theravada remained conservative to the point of an almost fundamentalist adherence to the early Pali texts,[38] Mahayana was liberal in practically every respect. It accepted later texts as equally authoritative, was less strict in interpreting disciplinary rules, and held a higher regard for the spiritual

---

[38] Pali: the traditional literary language of India in which the Hinayana canon was written.

possibilities of women and less-gifted monks as well as laymen generally.

In conclusion, it is interesting to note that the religion which began as a revolt against rites, rituals, grace, speculation, supernaturalism, and a human soul ends with all the excluded elements reinstated. And the founder who was regarded as an atheist in respect to belief in a personal God is ultimately transmogrified into that very type of God himself.

The Buddhism of Sri Lanka, Burma, Cambodia, and Thailand is Theravada. The Buddhism of China, Japan, and Korea is Mahayana. The geographical alignment has led some scholars to designate the former as "Southern" and the latter as "Northern."

Why Buddhism Failed in India

Buddhism today is present in practically every Asian land except India. After all, it was in India where it began; why, then, did it fail to root itself there?

Until about 1000 A.D. Buddhism continued in India as a distinct movement. Its differences with Hinduism have since softened. Hinduism recognized in the course of time the need for those reforms which Buddha had championed. The reforms that were initiated blurred the distinction between the Buddhism of India and the religion it had protested against, Hinduism. In other words, the Buddhism of India merged back into the historical stream from which it had arisen.

Mahayana's Mystical View of Reality

Mahayana Buddhism posits an absolute which

transcends knowing and being. Nothing can be affirmed of it, not even that it is, for existence and non-existence are relative terms one of which supports the other. No significant name can be given to it, but since a term is necessary for referring to it, it is called "the empty" (void of definable content), as we speak of "the absolute" (free from all relations). Another term that is used is *Bhutatathata*, "that which is such as it is" (cannot be compared to anything else). The phenomenal world is a manifestation of the absolute in seeming finiteness, manifoldness, and changefulness. This seeming arises from ignorance, and the ignorance is not merely subjective—the inborn realism of the human mind—but is potentially in the absolute. Being a pure negation, it is held to be not incompatible with the monistic premises.

The absolute in itself is above consciousness, which implies individuation (personality); the principle of individuation is ignorance. When we are confronted with the question as to how the unconscious absolute through ignorance comes to consciousness, the unconditioned becomes conditioned, there is nothing for it but to say "spontaneously"—that is, not with reason and purpose. Corresponding to the two aspects of the absolute are two forms of knowledge, transcendental and relative, the knowledge of the unconditioned and of the conditioned.[39] So long as we remain in ignorance, the world as it is for us and we ourselves with our self-consciousness have a relative reality. However, once ignorance is overcome, then the illusory reality vanishes, and there remains only the absolute that is what it is.

---

[39] The same distinction is made in the Vedanta philosophy, to which the whole system is closely related.

The Closeness of Mahayana's Personal and
Transcendent God Concept to Hinduism's

As the Vedanta has not only its transcendent Brahman without attributes but also its Brahman with
attributes, personal god, an object of religious devotion, so Mahayana Buddhism has, beside its ontologi-
cal absolute, the conception of a supreme being endowed
with all perfections. Intelligence, will, and above all
love are not mere attributes but the very essence of this
being. The commonest, and apparently the oldest,
name for this being is *Dharmakaya*, often translated
"Body of the Law" (i.e., religion). The protean senses of
Dharma make every interpretation uncertain; or rather
make it certain that those who used the name found in
it different meanings. Dharmakaya, the ground of
being, the one true reality, is not somewhere, but everywhere in the universe; the finite and fragmentary consciousness of individuals is a partial manifestation of
the universal intelligence.

The Buddhas are, in an eminent sense, manifestations or incarnations of the Dharmakaya; in a later
time even the word *avatara* is used, as of the incarnations of Vishnu, doubtless under the influence of Vish-
nuite notions. The motive of the incarnation is love; the
compassion which fills the heart of the Bodhisattva for
the suffering of beings who in their ignorance, think
thoughts, cherish desires, perform acts whose consequences they must suffer from existence to existence is
in God an infinite compassion, and moves him to seek
the salvation of all. Sakyamuni, who is referred to as
the historical Buddha, was such a manifestation of the
Dharmakaya. After his entrance into Nirvana he did
not cease to be Buddha; the love and devotion of those
who through him had found salvation have their
transcendental expression in an eternal Buddhahood.

A further advance in Buddhology is the doctrine of the *Trikaya* ("Three Bodies"). Every Buddha may be contemplated within three forms.

Hinduism asserts that there are three levels of divine beings. The highest is the paramatman, or world soul; next is the level of the *Tri-murti*, or secondary manifestations of the ultimate; and finally the incarnate savior gods, or avatars, who live among men for their salvation. This is closely parallel to the scheme of the three levels and three bodies of the Buddhas in Mahayana Buddhism:

1. The Dhyani Buddhas. These possess a *dharmakaya* or absolute body. They are "Buddhas of meditation" and have entered Nirvana forever, never again to have contact with the world of space and time. This corresponds with the paramatman of Hinduism.

2. The Bodhisattva possess a *Sambhogakaya*, body of bliss. This corresponds to the level of the Hindu god Vishnu, for though they reside in paradise they have the power to come to the aid of men.

3. The Manushi Buddhas, or human Buddhas, possess a *nirmanakaya*, or body of transformation. These Buddhas have lived among men, as did Siddhartha Gautama, and are comparable to Krishna as the avatar of Vishnu. Once a Manushi Buddha has performed his allotted task, he enters Nirvana and can no longer be of any help to men.

Although this view of the deity may be difficult for the average Buddhist to fathom, nevertheless it is basic to Mahayana theology.

Mahayana's Mystical Concept of Salvation

According to the Mahayanists, there are two levels of

salvation, a lower and a higher. The lower level offers man help if he turns to the Bodhisattvas, beings who have achieved Buddhahood, but have refused to enter Nirvana until all who seek their help precede them.

The higher level parallels that of the way of knowledge in Hinduism. In it, in the midst of time and space; eternity is to be found by those who follow the path of knowledge and grasp the true meaning of existence. They can experience the peace of Nirvana in the midst of time.

Adi-Buddha: Head of the Spiritual Hierarchy

The Mahayanists, like their forebears, the Hindus, have a host of gods, with one Supreme head whom they call Adi-Buddha who is regarded as the creator and essence of the universe. Under this creator, corresponding closely to Parabrahma of classical Hinduism, the Mahayanists describe five distinct Buddhas each with his successive incarnations. The relation of the five Buddhas to the transcendent creator, Adi-Buddha, approximates those of the Hindu gods Vishnu and Shiva in their different avatars with the deity of Ishvara.

The five Buddhas function successively on three different planes on their way down from their proximity to the divine effulgence of the Adi-Buddha to actual incarnation in a human form. The names of the five Buddhas are: Vairochana, Akshobya, Ratnasambhava, Amogudasiddha, and Amitabha; this last one is the historical Buddha, Siddhartha Gautama. Each of these Buddhas assumes three persons, corresponding to the three planes on which they function, on their way from their exalted glory to the lowly plane of concrete incarnation.

The five Buddhas next to Adi-Buddha are known as Dhyani Buddhas. They are responsible for engendering a Bodhisattva, a being who presides over the conditions necessary for the incarnation of a Buddha upon the earth. When all the terrestrial conditions are present, the Bodhisattva assumes a human body and appears as a savior of mankind. Thus, when Amitabha directed his creative energies towards an incarnation in the human form, he first became the *Avalokiteshvara*, the compassionate one, whose infinite benevolence is symbolized in his statues by numerous arms with open hands pouring his blessings upon the world. In the course of time Avalokiteshvara left the causal plane to incarnate on earth as the *Sakyamuni*, Siddhartha Gautama.

Buddhist mysticism was inspired by the idea of an all-pervading creative essence personified in the figure of Adi-Buddha; the most exalted aspect of Atta, the Hindu atma; and by the continuity of essential beings through the process of incarnations.

The interest in mysticism was intensified by the teaching that the illumination of subliminal consciousness attained by the Buddha which allowed Him to merge His nature with the pure light of the One Reality—is accessible to all men.

For the Chinese and other Eastern Asiatics, among whom are to be found the greatest number of Mahayanists, this possibility for all men to obtain liberating illumination became the most important aspect of Buddhism. It made Mahayana Buddhism a most fertile soil for the growth of Buddhist mysticism.

Degrees of Dhyana (Meditation) in Preparation
for a Mystical Experience

The Dhyana of Buddhism is a means employed by an
individual seeking a mystical experience. The meditation starts with a simple discipline of the mind and
control of the emotions. It leads to a state of felicity and
enlightenment. It ends in a sublime union with the
Supreme—referred to by Buddhists as being "the fullness of the void."

Buddhists describe four degrees of Dhyana. The first
degree is one of complete concentration on a chosen
object. It is accompanied by a feeling of serenity which
is derived by detachment from earthly illusions. In this
case the mind is still active and fixed on the object of
concentration.

In the second degree of Dhyana, the concentration
on the chosen object is replaced by intuitive contemplation. This brings the mind to a state of peace through
the cessation of its activity. The entire being experiences a deep feeling of joy.

In the third degree of Dhyana, objectivity is totally
transcended, objects disappear, the individual finds
himself or herself in a state of indifference to all emotions of pleasure or displeasure. The mind in this state
is freed from all passion and desire.

The fourth degree of Dhyana produces a state in
which consciousness of the present and memories of
the past disappear. In this state true serenity is
achieved. It is a purely transcendent state; it is the
state in which the individual is merged, so to speak,
with the Supreme.

Why There Are Few Accounts of
Buddhist Mystical Experiences

Although mystical experiences among Buddhists in
the form of ecstasies and illuminations are not a rare
occurrence, accounts of such experiences are fewer
than a Westerner might expect. Two reasons are given
for this phenomenon: one is objective, and the other
subjective. The objective reason is the Mahayanist's
conception of the impersonality of the Supreme Reality. This conception precludes any attempt on the part
of the mystic to report on spiritual experiences in the
form of personal images or depictable representations.

The subjective reason for the rare appearance of
ecstatic rhapsodies in Buddhist writings is psychological in nature. Buddhist mystics, with few exceptions,
claim that the rapturous joy which comes to them from
the eradication of the limitation of the ordinary self-
centered consciousness is but a mere inkling of the
really transcendent states. The urge, therefore, to describe the intermediary stages with all their profound
felicity and glorious visions disappears. In addition,
the Buddhist mystic, perhaps unlike other mystics,
fears that the enjoyment of his experience may cause
delay in the dissolution of all fetters, thus impeding
him in his flight to the Infinite. However, if Buddhist
literature fails to offer us the expected mystical effu-
sions, Buddhist hagiography compensates us with
abundant proofs of an intense mystical activity
throughout the ages.

While Buddhism considers mystical trances and
ecstasies as but merely transitory steps leading to the
complete liberation from the unreal, having no intrinsic value, Buddhist mystics nevertheless make a significant contribution to the mystical world by their

glorification of the human faculty with which one reaches states of consciousness far transcending those that are attainable by the senses.

Concluding Note on Buddhism and Buddhist Mysticism

As I see it, it is not only the Mahayana branch of Buddhism that meets the mystical requirements, believing in a god and a soul, but the religion of Buddhism as a whole, despite the denial of a god and a soul by the Theravadins. For both the Mahayanists and the Theravadins have a common, paramount aim, and that is to achieve Nirvana.

The members of the former branch wish to achieve it partially during their existence. The members of the latter branch aim to attain it in its complete form, which represents full release from the physical aspects of life or total extinguishment.

But Nirvana, some will surely contend, is not the Absolute and the *skandhas* (the body, sensations, perceptions, predispositions, and consciousness) regarded by the Theravadins as the essence of man are not the soul. How then can these concepts be equated? The answer to the question can only be given by another question: What precisely is meant by the concept of the Absolute and the concept of the soul? If these concepts could be defined on a universal basis, then perhaps the difference between Nirvana and the Absolute and the *skandhas* and the soul would not appear so strikingly different.

However, since clear, comprehensive definitions of the terms are unavailable, are beyond human ken to coin, and since both the individuals who are striving to unite with the Absolute and those who are intent on attaining Nirvana are inspired by the same aim, which is achieving genuine inner peace, perhaps there is no harm in regarding the Nirvanists, if I may call them so, as mystics equal to the Absolutists.

In preparation for their goal they both try to shape their lives in a manner that will lead them to it and render them worthy of it.

Buddhism, governed primarily by the principle of Nirvana, is, to my way of thinking, a religion that is wholly mystical in its nature.

Chapter Four

Jewish Mysticism

Mysticism is man's recognition of
the presence of a particle of the
"Over Soul" within him.

S.U.

The Origin and Meaning of the Term *Kabbala*

 rior to the introduction of the term *Kab-bala*, its doctrine was known as *hochmah nistrarah* ("hidden wisdom") and its followers were referred to as *yordeh merkabah* ("riders of the chariot").

At a later time, the term Kabbala was

adopted instead of using the expression "hidden wisdom." The word Kabbala means "tradition," "transmitted teachings." It is the term used for Jewish speculations on the mysteries of God and the universe.

Kabbalistic lore derives neither from revelation nor
from science but from individual mystic speculations
on the part of its votaries. The results of such speculation become esoteric, or hidden, in the sense that they
are transmitted to the initiated, who alone are considered capable of understanding and communicating
them.

Theories on the Origin of the Kabbala

Theories as to the origin of the Kabbala date its
beginnings as early as remote antiquity or as late as
the 13th and 14th centuries. Its doctrines, it is believed,
were derived from Egypt, Babylonia, Plato, Neoplatonism, the categories of Aristotle, the philosophic mysticism of Philo, and early Christian Gnosticism.

It may be stated, however, that the roots of the Kabbala are laid fairly deep, and that its history antedates
by many centuries the literature that expresses its
theories.

For centuries thoughts and ideas embodied in the
Kabbala have been present in the consciousness of the
Jewish people, filling their lives with an overmastering
nearness of God, an assurance of His interest in their
daily concerns. It was this sense of the reality of God,
and their seeking communion with Him, that gave the
great characters of the Old Testament a unique quality. In no other literature are such ardent, mystical
longings for the divine to be found.

Early Jewish Mysticism

Religion, in order that it should not be barren and
lifeless, must give prominence to something more than
ritual, tradition, and certain observances. It must lay
stress on the element of personal, inward experiences,
on the great fact of the soul "athirst for God, yea even
for the living God." Judaism amply fulfills these
conditions.

The beginnings of Judaism lie, of course, in the Old
Testament. In fact, everything in Judaism seeks to find
its confirmation in some expression, whether clear or
veiled, in the Old Testament. Hence the Old Testament
is important for any consideration of Jewish mysticism in all its phases and developments.

The mysticism of the Old Testament clusters mostly
around the visionary experiences of the prophets. Isai-
ah's vision of a God whose "train filled the Temple"
points to the all-inclusiveness of the Deity. Ezekiel's
fits of ecstasy are characteristic of the mood of many a
mystic in all ages. Some of the other books of the Old
Testament show forth other constituents of the mystical consciousness. Thus, the Psalmists often brood on
the divinity manifested in the beauteous world of
nature: "Who layeth the beams of his upper chambers
in the waters; who maketh the cloud his chariot; who
walketh upon the wings of the wind. Who maketh
winds his messenger; his ministers flaming fire."[40]

Psalm 139: 1-13 portrays the mystic sense of the
boundless, and the human aspiration to reach it as the
goal of the truest safety from the ills and anxieties of
the normal finite experience. Other passages point to
the 'nearness' of God and the joys of intimate converse
with Him.

---

[40] Ps. 104:3-4.

The treatment of prayer and the specimens given of individual prayers are fine examples of what one might call "erotic mysticism." The soul passionately yearns for God, and God reciprocates the yearning in terms of the love between man and woman. "Whom have I in heaven but thee? and there is none upon earth that I desire besides thee."[41] Here is the insatiable craving of the mystic, the infinity of love's desire. "Yea I have loved thee with an everlasting love; therefore with loving kindness have I drawn thee."[42] All these expressions represent an outpouring of living religion to which the name mysticism may rightly be applied.

Esoteric Sects

Another instance of early Jewish mysticism is the presence in Palestine of a number of esoteric sects in the 2nd century B.C. Two of the more popular of the sects were the Essenes and the *Vatikin* ("men of firm principles").

Of the Essenes Philo Judaeus writes: "Of natural philosophy. . .they study only that which pertains to the existence of God and the beginning of all things; otherwise they devote all their attention to ethics, using as instructors the laws of their fathers, which, without the outpouring of the Divine Spirit, the human mind could not have devised. . .for, following their ancient traditions, they obtain their philosophy by means of allegorical interpretations. . . . Of the love of God they exhibit myriads of examples, inasmuch as they strive for continued uninterrupted life of purity and holiness; they avoid swearing and falsehood, and

---

[41]   Ps. 73:25.
[42]   Jer. 31:3.

they declare that God causes only good and no evil whatsoever.... No one possesses a house absolutely as his own, one which does not at the same time belong to all; for in addition to living in companies, their houses are open also to their adherents coming from other quarters. They have one storehouse for all, and the same diet; their garments belong to all in common, and their meals are taken in common."[43]

The mysticism of the *Vatikin* seems to have clustered mostly round the sentiments and outward conduct governing prayers. They were a brotherhood whose dominant feature was simplicity of living combined with a degree of earnest scrupulousness in prayer amounting to an adoration, a love of the Divine such as is experienced by the mystics of all times everywhere.

Philo and Jewish Mysticism

In the early centuries of the Christian era, according to modern research, there was a certain degree of inter-course between Jewish scholars of Palestine and Baby-lonia on the one hand, and the Jewish scholars of Alexandria on the other, Alexandria having been the great center of Hellenistic culture. This no doubt resulted in an interchange of ideas and doctrines which in time found their way into the literatures of both branches.

An example of this intermingling of ideas is the phi-losophy of the famous Philo Judaeus of Alexandria, which consisted of a fusion of Platonic, Stoic, and Rab-binic strata.

In Jewish mysticism Philo is noted for his Logos idea. The Logos idea was his response to the question of

---

[43] Philo Judaeus, *The Contemplative Life*, ed. F.C. Conybeare (Oxford, 1895), pp. 53, 206.

how at the creation of man it was possible for God, who is the all-holy and the all-perfect, to come into contact with imperfect man.

The Midrashic answer to the question—the answer of the Hebrew scholars—was that God did not really come into contact with impure man or an impure world, but that His angels did, and that His angels are really part and parcel of His own being, emanations of His substance. This was, of course, far from a logical solution.

Philo's answer to the question of how the all-holy, all-perfect could come in contact with impure man and an impure world was similar to the answer given by the Hebrew scholars. He says, "For God, not condescending to come down to the external senses, sends His own *logoi* [words]. . . ."[44]

The angels, as the representatives of God of which the Hebrew scholars speak, and the *Logoi* (Words), of which Philo speaks, have very much the same nature and fulfill very much the same function.

As the Hebrew scholars or rabbis talked of angels as God's representatives and also attributed personality to them, so Philo talked of Logoi as God's representatives on earth and gave them personality. Hence the angels of the rabbis are the personified Logoi of Philo.

Philo describes the personified Logos as the being who guided the patriarchs, as the angel who appeared before Hagar, as God's ambassador to the human race, as an attendant on the Supreme being, and as a paraclete. "For it was indispensable that the man who was consecrated to the Father of the world should have, as a paraclete, his son, the being most perfect in virtue, to procure forgiveness of sins, and a supply of unlimited blessings."[45]

---

44   Philo, *On Dreams* i. 12.
45   Philo, *Life of Moses* iii. 14.

It is to the figure of Metatron that rabbinic mysticism turns to as a counterpart to the personified Logos of Philo. "Behold I send an angel before thee to keep thee in the way and to bring thee into the place which I have prepared. Beware of him and obey his voice, provoke him not; for he will not pardon your transgressions; *for my name is in him.*"[46] This angel in whom God's name exists is, said the rabbis, Metatron. And why so? Because, said they, the numerical value of the Hebrew letters composing the name Metatron (314) corresponds with those comprising the word *Shaddai* (Almighty, one of the Divine appellations).

This illustration is typical of the rabbinic mysticism clustering around (i) arithmetical numbers and (ii) the Divine name. "My name is in him" i.e., the name "Almighty" is comprehended in the name "Metatron." And the Divine name is not merely a grammatical part of speech. It is a kind of essence of the Deity Himself. Hence the essence of the Deity exists in Metatron. He is God's lieutenant. He represents the active phase of the Deity as manifested in the universe.

Metatron in Jewish mysticism is viewed as a link uniting the human with the Divine, the bridge over which the knowledge of what is passing here below is brought to the realms above, and over which, in return, the Divine concern for men and the world passes down to the scenes of earth.

Metatron has been identified with the Zoroastrian Mithra.

Jewish Mysticism in the Apocrypha and Talmud

In the 2nd century B.C., the writer Ben Sira warned against overindulgence in mystical speculation. He

---

[46] Exodus 23: 20-21.

writes, "Thou shalt have no business with secret things,"[47] and there are many indications of its exist-ence in the Apocrypha and Pseudepigrapha, notably the Enoch books and the testament of various Biblical heroes.

As for mystical speculation in the Talmud, it is indi-cated that the imagination of the rabbis was especially stirred when they studied those portions of Genesis dealing with creation, which they called *Maaseh Bere-shith* (History of Creation) and the visions of Ezekiel 1 and 10, containing the description of the *Merkabah*, the divine chariot, which they called *Maaseh Mer-kabah* (History of the Divine Throne).

As early as the 3rd and 4th centuries A.D. mystic speculation in Palestine was very much in evidence. How widely diffused the interest in occult science must have been may be deduced from the disturbance the rabbis felt about the growing absorption of scholars in mysticism and the attempts they made to discourage it.[48]

In the Talmud, a number of *Tannaim* are named who busied themselves with the mysteries of theosophical speculation. Included are: Johanan ben Zakkai and his disciple Joshua ben Hananiah, Akiba, Ben Zoma, Ben Azzai, and Elisha ben Abuyah. Of these last four it is said that they entered the "garden" (*Pardes*), a name used by mystics referring to the mystical teachings. As a result of these teachings, it is reported that Ben Zoma became insane; Ben Azzai died young; Elisha ben Abuyah turned heretic; only Akiba entered the "garden" in peace and departed in peace.[49]

This story proves not only the widespread preval-

---

[47]　Sirach 3:22.

[48]　*Hag.* 2:1; 13a.

[49]　*Hag.* 14b.

ence and mysteriousness of the secret lore, but also the terror in which it was held.

Sepher Yetzirah (*The Book of Creation*)

The *Book of Creation* had the widest possible influence on the development of the Kabbala and at the beginning of the 9th century enjoyed so great a reputation that no less a man than the famous Jewish philosopher Saadia ben Joseph (892-942) translated it into Arabic and wrote a commentary on it.

The interest in the book is derived from the fact that, for the first time, a history of cosmogony is attempted in terms of numbers.

The book, it is thought by scholars, appeared in the 6th century A.D., and is believed to be the work of several authors. It consists of a mystical philosophy drawn from the sounds, shapes, and numerical values of the letters of the Hebrew alphabet. All the twenty-two letters play a dominant role in the book's philosophy.

It says: "By means of twenty-two letters, by giving them a form and a shape, by mixing them and combining them in different ways, God made the soul of all that which has been created and of all that which will be. It is upon these same letters that the Holy One has founded His high and holy Name" (ii.2).

The cosmos—embraced in the twenty-two letters—is an expression of the Divine intelligence. Man, the world, time—these three constitute the cosmos, and outside them there is but one great existence, the Infinite. This brings us to two doctrines of Jewish mysticism which appear for the first time in the *Book of*

Creation. These are: (a) the doctrine of emanation; (b) the Ten *Sefiroth.*

Emanation implies that all existing things are successive outflowings of God, that God contains within Himself all. He is perfect, incomprehensible, indivisible, dependent on nothing, in need of nothing. Everything in the cosmos, all finite creatures animate and inanimate, flow out, radiate, in a successive series from God, the Perfect One. This teaching raises a question. How can there be any connecting link between a Being who is infinite, changeless, and perfect and matter which is finite, changeable, and imperfect? All doctrines answer the question in more or less the same way by saying that God is not really external to anyone or anything. Everything is originally comprehended in Him, "with no contrasts here or there, no oppositions of this and that, no separation into change and variation."[50] On this understanding there is no necessity for hunting after "the missing link" between the Divine and the human.

The multiplicity that one beholds in the cosmos, all things that make up the universe, are emanations from the one Unity, manifestations of the God from whom all things flow and to whom they must all finally return because they are ultimately one with the One, just as the flame is one with the candle from which it issues.

In the *Book of Creation* the teaching about emanation is intertwined with the doctrine of the Ten Sefiroth, which in all probability originated with the rabbis of the Talmud in the first three centuries of the Christian era. Thus, a passage in *T. B. Haggigah* speaks of the "ten agencies through which God created

---

[50]   Rufus M. Jones, *Studies in Mystical Religion* (London: 1909), p. 13.

the world; *viz.*, wisdom, insight, cognition, strength, power, inexorableness, justice, right, love, mercy."[51]

Now, what, according to the *Book of Creation*, is the relation between the cosmic powers of the twenty-two letters of the Hebrew alphabet and the cosmic parts played by the Ten Sefiroth? The Ten Sefiroth, according to the book, are the categories of the universe, the forms or molds into which all created things were originally cast. They are form, as distinguished from matter. Whereas the Sefiroth are responsible for the first production of form, so the twenty-two letters are the prime cause of matter. All existence and development are due to the creative powers of the letters, but they are inconceivable apart from the *form* with which the Sefiroth have invested them.

Through the letters and the Sefiroth, the *Book of Creation* teaches that God and the world are a unity rather than a duality. The Sefiroth and the twenty-two letters of the alphabet—or, in other words, the forms and essences which make up the visible universe—are all an unfolding of the Divine, all emanations from the Spirit. God is at one and the same time both the matter and form of the universe. But He is also something more. He is not identical with the universe. He is greater than it. He transcends it. Nothing exists or can exist outside Him. Though immanent, He is also at the same time transcendent.

The naive conception of the mysterious powers of the letters and numbers set forth in the *Book of Creation*, in the medieval period was eventually superseded by the introduction of theological and moral ideas. The object of discussion became not so much the relationship between the Creator and His cosmos as the relationship between God and that inner surging world

---

[51] *Hag.* 12a.

of thought and emotion which we term man. How man can ascend to God whilst bound in the trammels of the flesh, and how God communicates Himself to man— these themes are generally presented in the *Zohar*.

The *Zohar*

The *Zohar* (literally "Shining" or "Brightness," from the words in Daniel 21:3, "And they that be wise shall shine as the brightness of the firmament") is the text-book of Jewish medieval mysticism. The *Zohar* is more of a library than a single book, a quintessence of all that Jews felt and thought upon the subject of the Kabbala at different times and places.

The Date and Authorship of the *Zohar*

The *Zohar* pretends to be the record of a direct Divine revelation to Rabbi Simeon ben Yohai of the 2nd century in Galilee. Criticism, however, has long ago demonstrated the utter untenability of this view. The *Zohar* made its first appearance in the 13th century in Spain, and its contents show indisputably that not only must the work be considerably later than the 2nd century, but that it could not possibly be the production of a single author or a single period of history. The book, like the *Book of Creation*, is a syncretism. Many civilizations, many faiths, and many philosophies went into the making of it.

The Popularity of the *Zohar*

The *Zohar* was like a torch set to dry wood, for no sooner had it made its appearance than it became the most popular book of Jewish mystics of all lands. Even those who could not follow its theology were attracted by its picturesque style and fantastic explanation of Biblical texts.

The Contents of the *Zohar*

The group of Kabbalistic works which make up the *Zohar* literature is divided into three separate books which were published at different times. These are the *Zohar* proper, the *Zohar Hadash* ("The New *Zohar*"), and the *Tikkune ha Zohar* ("The Explanations or Additions to the *Zohar*"). However, what we call the *Zohar* proper is by no means a homogeneous work but a heterogeneous one. It contains the largest number of the parts of the group. It consists of (1) the *Saphra di Zenuita* ("The Book of Secrecy"), a booklet of only three pages, written in enigmatic language and considered as the source and nucleus of the entire *Zohar*; (2) the *Idra Rabba* ("The Large Assembly") called thus because it contains the teachings revealed at an assembly of initiates presided over by Simeon ben Yohai, primarily a commentary on the *Saphra di Zenuita*, although it contains many other additions; (3) the *Idra Zuta* ("The Small Assembly"), containing the teachings supposed to have been revealed by Simeon ben Yohai immediately before his death, when the number of initiates present was smaller (three of the original group had already passed away); (4) the *Zohar* to the section of creation, i.e., the first section of Genesis, though really a part of

the entire mystic Midrash to the Pentateuch, originally
a separate book written prior to the entire Midrash; (5)
the *Midrash Zohar* to the Pentateuch, containing discussions of a philosophical, theological, and Aggadic
nature together with mystic teachings; (6) the *Sitre
Torah* ("The Mysteries of the Torah"), a collection of
passages which deal primarily with mystic teachings
regarding the soul, angels, the secrets of the alphabet
letters, and the names of God; (7) the *Ra'aya Mehemna*
("The Faithful Shepherd"), a work which intends to
explain the precepts in a Kabbalistic way, the author
endeavoring to find a hidden meaning in every precept
or commandment (*Mitzvah*); (8) the *Midrash ha Nea-
lam* ("The Hidden Midrash"), dealing primarily with
allegorical interpretations of verses and passages in
the Book of Genesis, its teachings centering around the
problem of the soul and its destiny in the hereafter and
(9) the *Raza di Razin* ("The Secret of Secrets"), a small
booklet devoted primarily to the problem of physiog-
nomy, develops an entire system of signs and features
by means of which the character of a man can be
determined and his future foretold.

The *Zohar Hadash* ("The New *Zohar*") consists of
three different parts. It contains, first of all, additions
to the *Zohar* on different sections of the Pentateuch as
well as various recensions of passages contained in the
old *Zohar*. Second, it includes large fragments of the
two mystic works *Midrash ha-Nealam* and *Raza di
Razin*. Third, it comprises three small *Zohar Midra-
shim* to Canticles, Ruth, and Lamentations.

The *Tikkunim* are a collection of additions to the
Zohar in the *Bereshith* ("creation") section of Genesis.
They are so called because they are further explana-
tions to the teachings given in that part of the *Zohar*.

The doctrines contained in the *Zohar* are taken to be
the Kabbala. The *Zohar* is both the complete guide of

the different Kabbalistic theories and the canonical book of the Kabbalists.

The compilers of the *Zohar* made extensive use of the natural sciences as they were known at that time. There are so many physiological passages which bear evidence of a fair acquaintance with the functions of the organs of the body. There are also a number of scientific maxims quoted in the various parts of the work, among them the famous Aristotelian maxim "Nature does not make any leaps" (*Natura saltum non facit*). Very remarkable is the passage in the *Zohar* which discloses a knowledge of the rotation of the earth around the sun. It is quoted in the name of the book of Rabbi Hamnuna Saba and reads as follows: "The earth revolves in a circle like a ball; some of the inhabitants are below and some are above. All the creatures differ in their looks in accordance with the change of the climate. There are places on the earth where there is light when the opposite places are in the dark. In other words, there is day in one place when there is night in another. There is one place where the day lasts for almost the entire twenty-four hours, except for a very short time of darkness."[52] The author of the quoted passage no doubt received the information he is giving from Arabic sources which recounted the various ancient theories about the world. All the statements show a wide acquaintance with astronomical data.

After the *Zohar*, which must be dated at about the beginning of the 14th century, and which received its present shape largely from the hand of Moses de Leon, a period of pause ensued in the development of the Kabbala which lasted for more than two and a half centuries.

---

[52] *Zohar*, Pt. iii, 10a.

The Language of the *Zohar*

The language of the *Zohar* is not only strong and powerful but highly poetic. Figures of speech and similes abound. Picture and symbol are the very warp and woof of all mystic literature and the *Zohar* is most typical of its kind.

The Ten Sefiroth of the *Zohar*

All existences are emanations from the Deity. The Deity reveals Himself in all existences because He is immanent in them. But, though dwelling in them, He is greater than they. He is apart from them. He transcends them. "He is at the same time the most Hidden of the hidden. He is separated from all things, and is at the same time not separated from all things. For all things are united in Him, and He unites Himself with all things. There is nothing which is not in Him. He has a shape, and one can say that he has not one. In assuming a shape, He has given existence to all things. He made ten lights spring forth from His midst, lights which shine with the form which they have borrowed from Him, and which shed everywhere the light of a brilliant day. The Infinite, the Holy One, the most Hidden of the hidden, is a high beacon, and we know Him only by His lights. His Holy name is no other thing than these lights."[53]

The "ten lights" are, of course, the Ten Sefiroth, the ten successive emanations from the Godhead, the ten

---

[53] From a passage in the *Zohar* called *Idra Zuta* ("Small Assembly").

powers or qualities which were latent from all eternity in the Godhead.[54]

The first of the Ten Sefiroth is the Crown (*Keter* in Hebrew). The Crown is the first of the emanations from the Infinite (*En-Sof*). The Crown represents the first stage by which the Infinite Being takes on the properties of the finite and becomes drawn out of His impenetrable isolation. But nevertheless, the Crown is an absolute indivisible unity, possessing no attributes or qualities, baffling all analysis and description. The Crown may be said to be "pure being." It is the starting point of everything. It is the thought of God—the plan of the universe.

Wisdom and Intelligence are the second and third of the Ten Sefiroth. "When the Ancient One, the Holy One, desired to bring all things into being, He created them all as male and female."[55] Wisdom is the "father," the masculine active principle which engenders all things and imposes on them form and measure. Intelligence is the "mother," the passive, receptive principle. Out of the union of Wisdom and Intelligence comes a "son" who is dowered with the characteristics of both parents. The son is Reason (*Daath*). These three, father, mother, and son, hold and unite in themselves all that which has been, which is, and which will be. But they in turn are all united to the first Sefirah (the Crown), who is the all-comprehensive One who is, was, and will be.

The first three Sefiroth form a triad constituting the world as a manifestation of the Divine Thought. The

[54] The Sefiroth of the *Book of Creation* differ from those of the *Zohar* and the medieval Kabbala generally in one cardinal respect; whereas in the two latter systems the Sefiroth have the fullest possible mystical connotations, in the *Book of Creation* they cluster mainly around the mysticism of numbers.

[55] *Zohar*, Pt. iii, 290a.

remaining seven Sefiroth likewise fall into triads.
From the union of Mercy and Justice the result is
Beauty. Mercy is the active, masculine principle, is the
life-giving, ever-forgiving power in man and the universe. Justice holds back what would otherwise prove
to be the excess of Mercy.

The third triad is Victory, Glory, and Foundation.
The first of these is the masculine principle. The second
is the feminine, passive principle. The third, Foundation, is the effect of the combination of Victory and
Glory. These two allude to the dynamic aspect of the
universe, the ceaseless, developing world.

The last of the Sefiroth is Royalty. The tenth Sefirah
indicates the abiding truth of the harmonious coopera-
tion of all the Sefiroth, thus making the universe in its
orderliness and in its symmetry a true and exact manifestation of the Divine Mind.

The fact that all the Sefiroth fall into triads or trini-
ties and that ascribed to them are such titles as
"father," "mother," and "son" has encouraged many
apologists for Christianity to say that the essential
Christian dogma of the Trinity is implicit in Jewish
mystical literature.

The *Zohar* on the Soul

The *Zohar*, like Plotinus, draws a distinction between
lower souls (those who would act corruptly in the
world) and higher souls; it, unlike Plotinus, makes
every soul descend into some body. Plotinus has a different view.

The lower soul desires a body and lives in the stage of
sense. . . . The higher soul, on the other hand, tran-

scends the body, "rides upon it" as the fish is in the sea or as the plant is in the air. This higher soul never absolutely leaves its home, its *being* is not here but "yonder" or, in the language of Plotinus, "The soul always leaves something of itself above."[56]

According to the *Zohar*—which also makes distinctions between superior and inferior souls, as shown by their belonging to a higher or lower Sefirah—they must all descend to earth and unite with the body and all return at death to their fountainhead, God.

The *Zohar* describes the soul as a trinity. It comprises three elements: (a) *Neshamah*, the rational element which is the highest phase of existence; (b) *Ruah*, the moral element, the seat of good and evil, the ethical qualities; (c) *Nefesh*, the gross side of spirit, the vital element which is *en rapport* with the body, and the mainspring of all movements, instincts, and cravings of the physical life.

The *Neshamah*, which is the soul in its most elevated and sublimest sense, emanated from the Sefirah of Wisdom. The *Ruah*, which denotes the soul in its ethical aspect, emanates from the Sefirah of Beauty. The *Nefesh*, which is the animal side of the soul, is an emanation from the Sefirah of Foundation, that element of divinity which comes in contact with the material forces of earth.

The three aspects of the human soul enable man to fit himself into the plan and framework of the cosmos, give him the power to perform his numerous duties towards the multifarious portions of the world, the world which is a manifestation of God's thought, a copy of the celestial universe, an emanation of the Divine.

---

[56] Jones, *Studies in Mystical Religion*, p. 74.

The three divisions or aspects of the *human soul form
only one* soul. The *Nefesh*, the lowest side of the soul,
does not in itself possess any light. This is why it is so
tightly joined to the body, acquiring for it the pleasures
and the foods which it needs. Above the *Nefesh* is the
Ruah [the ethical part of the soul], which dominates the
Nefesh, imposes laws upon it, and enlightens it as
much as nature requires. Then, high above the *Ruah* is
the *Neshamah*, which in its turn rules the *Ruah* and
sheds upon it the light of life. The *Ruah* is lit up by this
light and depends entirely upon it. . . . The *Neshamah* is
always climbing back again towards its source.[57]

The Soul's Symbol

The soul's most visible, most tangible, most perceiv-
able quality is love. The soul is the root of love. Love is
the symbol of the soul. The soul, says the mystic of all
ages, seeks to enter consciously into the presence of
God. It can do so only under the spur of an overpowering, ecstatic emotion called love.

Although, according to the *Zohar*, the soul in its most
exalted state as *Neshamah* can only enjoy the love
inherent in its union with its source after it has freed
itself from the contamination of earthly bodies, it is
nevertheless possible, under certain conditions, to
realize this ecstatic love while the soul is in the living
body of an individual. One of these conditions is *the act
of serving God*, the chief outward concomitant of
which is *prayer*.

"Whosoever serves God out of love," says the *Zohar*,
"comes into union with the place of the Highest of the
High, and comes into union too with the holiness of the

---

[57] *Zohar*, Pt. ii, 142.

world which is to be."[58] This is to say that the service of
God, when effected with love, leads the soul into union
with the place of its origin, and gives it, as it were, a
foretaste of the ineffable felicity which awaits it in its
highest condition as *Neshamah*.

The *Zohar* on the Transmigration of the Soul

The soul, as it descends from the upper worlds where
it originated, must by necessity return to its source, and
hence the importance of right conduct in human life.
The world is a school for the soul in which it is repeat-
edly tried, and by these trials it is elevated and per-
fected. The *Zohar* compares the sojourn of the soul of
the righteous on earth to the sojourn of a king's son in a
country far away from the royal palace. The prince was
sent there for special training, but when the training
was ended, the king sent the queen after him and she
brought the prince back to the palace.[59] Likewise, when
the time for the departure of the righteous from this
world arrives, a union of the king and queen occurs
again, i.e., the soul is returned to its source, it unites
with the king.

In connection with the views of the preexistence of
the soul and its sojourn on earth, the Kabbala introduced an exotic teaching into Judaism which ultimately became one of its important doctrines. This is
the doctrine of the transmigration of souls. This teaching was never sanctioned as a doctrine until the Kabbala incorporated it in its teaching.

To the minds of the Kabbalists, transmigration is a
necessity not alone on the grounds of their particular

---

58 *Zohar*, Pt. ii, 216.
59 *Zohar*, Pt. i, p. 245b.

theology—the soul must reach the highest stage of its evolution before it can be received again into its eternal home—but on moral grounds as well. It is a vindication of Divine justice to mankind. It settles the question which all ages have propounded: why does God permit the wicked to prosper, whereas the righteous man is allowed to reap nothing but sorrow? And the only way to reconcile the dismal fact of suffering with the belief in a good God is by saying that the pain is a retribution to the soul for sin committed in some one or more of its previous states.

A perfect condition of things will come only with the coming of the Messiah. Until that time, therefore, all souls, tainted as they inevitably are with sin, must by means of a chain of transmigrations from one body to another, shake off more and more of the dross clinging to them, until they reach that summit of purity and perfection when as *Neshamāh* they can find their way back to unite with the Infinite Source, the "Over-Soul."

The Kabbalist Isaac Luria (1534-72) added still another condition to the soul's ascent in a purified form to its Source. This condition is known as *Ibbur* ("Impregnation"). According to Luria's theory, if a single soul is not equal to the task appointed for it by heaven, then an additional soul is united with it so that they may support and complement each other. In that case, the stronger of the two souls becomes the mother of the weaker one, nursing it from her own substance, just as woman nurses a child.

The *Zohar* on Man

Man, as is known, holds a high position in all spiritual expressions of Judaism, in the Bible, the Talmud, and Agada. But in the Kabbala he attained his highest position. According to it, he is the very purpose of the entire creation, for does not his form represent the universe in being *"its scale or balance"* as the mystic doctrine teaches us?

The skin, says the *Zohar*, can be compared to the firmament which covers many things, and as in the firmament, the stars and planets in their formation and combination display certain signs by means of which the initiated can learn secrets, so does the skin possess such signs which reveal to those who know how to read them the secrets concerning the character and future of man.[60] These signs are, of course, the lines that cover the face and the palms of the hands and the formation of the nails.

Again, man, according to the *Zohar*, is a copy of the universe below as well as of the universe above. The *Zohar* puts it thus:

> Believe not that man consists solely of flesh, skin, bones, and veins. The real part of man is his soul, and the things just mentioned, the skin, flesh, bones, and veins, are only an outward covering, a veil, but are not the man.... The skin typifies the heavens which extend everywhere and cover everything like a garment. The flesh puts us in mind of the evil side of the universe. The bones and the veins symbolize the Divine chariot, the inner powers of man which are the servants of God. But they are all but an outer covering. For, inside man, there is the secret of the *Heavenly man*.... Everything below takes place in the same manner as everything above. This is the meaning of the remark that God created man in His own image. But just as in the heavens, which cover the whole universe, we behold different shapes brought about by the stars and the planets

---

[60] *Zohar*, Pt. ii, p. 76a, b.

to teach us concerning hidden things and deep secrets, so upon the skin which covers our body there are shapes and forms which are like planets and stars to our bodies. All these shapes have a hidden meaning and are observed by the sages who are able to read the face of man.[61]

Speculative and Practical Kabbala

The speculative aspect of Kabbala concerns itself with such problems as the nature of the Deity, the theory of Divine emanations, the creation of angels and man, their place and destiny in the world, the existence of evil, and the importance of the revealed Law.

Jewish thinkers and philosophers found it difficult to harmonize the creation and existence of the sensual world with the spiritual nature of God. The answers which Kabbala proposed to the questions that were raised about God, the universe, and man make up that aspect of the Kabbala which is termed speculative.

The practical aspect of the Kabbala was developed by Isaac Luria. It served as a response to those Jews for whom the theoretical or speculative Kabbala was no longer sufficient to satsify their spiritual needs. These Jews were looking for some mystic talisman with which to ease their pain. It was the time when many of them were still shocked and bewildered at their expulsion from Spain, where for centuries they had lived in peace and contributed to the enrichment of their own culture as well as the general culture of the land.

Isaac Luria provided his disturbed brethren with that which they were yearning for. He invented a

---

[61] *Zohar*, Pt. ii, 76a.

whole system of amulets, conjurations, mystic jugglery with words and numbers, and a process of ascetic practices by which the power of evil might be overcome. The use of Kabbala in this fashion is described as practical.

The Four Worlds of the Kabbala

As mentioned elsewhere in this chapter the introduction of the idea of the Sefiroth by the Kabbalists was for the purpose of explaining the relation between the Infinite (*En-Sof*) and the world of matter, of making them the mediators between the two. But the distance between the En-Sof and the world of matter is so great that the Sefiroth alone, which are highly spiritual powers or mere expressions of the substance of God, are not sufficient to fill the gap. There must be some links in the chain of being which affect its gradual thickening or materialization. A theory had been advanced, therefore, by the early Kabbalists that the Sefiroth represent only one world, that of *Aziluth* ("Emanation"), and that in addition there are three more worlds, that of *Beriah* ("Creation"), *Yetzira* ("Formation"), and *Asiyah* ("Action").

The underlying conception of the doctrine of the four worlds is that *being* in its various ramifications is one great unity permeated by the breath of God. The worlds or the great divisions of existence are all manifestations of the will or power of God. They all have one source. The difference between them is due to their distance from the source. The further the link is from the origin, the grosser and more material it becomes. But in all of the links, the light of the Sefiroth, the first emanation, flashes through. In general, we have to recognize not only a descending movement but also an ascending one. When materialization reached its lowest point in the grossest element, earth, an ascending movement set in, expressed by a desire on the part of all things to return to their origin. Thus the kingdom of plants represents a step higher than that of minerals, that of the animals another step, and that of man still another. Man himself represents many stages and expressions of that desire, and finally the process is completed in the return of the souls of the righteous to the source.

Jewish Mystics of the Medieval Period and Beyond

Azriel

Rabbi Azriel, also called Ezra (1160-1238), was born in Spain. He studied Jewish mysticism under Isaac the Blind. His influence on the development of the Kabbala was exceedingly great. He gave the doctrines he taught a philosophic coloring which rendered them more attractive to individuals of a philosophical bent. He authored a number of commentaries, the most important of which is the commentary on the Ten Sefiroth. Through this commentary Azriel attempts to show that all Kabbalistic teachings are grounded in the Bible and are not mere inventions of the mind.

Isaac Ibn Latif

Isaac Ibn Latif (1228-1290), of Toledo, Spain, was both a philosopher and a mystic and this combination is reflected in his works. He left a number of books of which the outstanding are: *Ginze ha-Melek* ("The

Treasures of the King"), the *Zurath Olam* ("The Form
of the World"), and the *Shaar ha-Shomayim* ("The Por-
tal of Heaven").

According to Latif, the first created being is an absolute, simple entity and the ground of all existing
things. In this process of emanation, the further a
being is in the scale of existence, the more material it
becomes. The number of separate intelligences is ten,
and these are the Sefiroth. The intelligences or Sefiroth
were the mediators through which the lower worlds
were created. Latif divides all existence into three
groups or worlds: the world of intelligences, the middle
world (i.e., the world of the spheres), and the world of
nature embracing all bodies in existence. And if we add
the first created being, which is the source of all these
worlds, we really have four worlds corresponding to a
certain extent to the system of the four worlds of the
Kabbala, though differing from it in important points.

Latif accepts emanation and the existence of the
Sefiroth, but he limits the process by positing a first
created being. He also employs to a great extent the
symbolism as well as the method of interpretation of
verses and the style of the Kabbala.

Latif's views represent an attempt to limit the teachings of the Kabbala and to guard that they do not
deviate from the fundamental doctrine of Judaism,
namely creation.

Moses de Leon

Moses de Leon (1250-1305) is the man whose name is
associated with bringing about the appearance of the
Zohar and who is often spoken of as its author. Moses
was born in Leon, Spain, but led a wandering life,

sojourning for periods in different cities. He was deeply immersed in the study of the Kabbala and possessed an encompassing knowledge of the entire field of mysticism. He is the author of a number of Kabbalistic works, one of which, *Shekel Hakodesh* ("The Holy Shekel"), is still extant in print.

Moses Cordevero

Moses Cordevero (1522-70) was born in Cordova, Spain, and later settled in Safed, Palestine. Cordevero was a productive writer and the number of his works is considerable. Besides writing several books on the Kabbala, he also wrote a long commentary on the *Zohar* under the title *Or Yakar* ("A Precious Light"). His great contribution to the Kabbala consists primarily of his systematization of its teachings in an orderly fashion. The crown of his works is his *Pardes Rimmonim* ("The Garden of Pomegrantes"). This book contains his complete Kabbalistic teachings. It deals practically with every phase of the Kabbala. Cordevero used profuse illustrations in his presentations which elucidate the most difficult points.

Cordevero had a large number of disciples in Safed, and many followers in all parts of the world who continued to expound his views after him.

Mystic Poets and Theologians

Solomon Ibn Gabirol

The poems of Solomon Ibn Gabirol (1021-1058) are imbued with mystical sentiment. The *Kether Mal-*

khuth ("Royal Crown") is one of the most beautiful descriptions ever penned of the truth of the Divine indwelling. The universe is composed of spheres one within the other; and the author's wealth of Biblical knowledge combined with his poet's education in the philosophy of Plotinus is used in showing how all the elements of earth and "every common sight" arouse the human heart to the feeling of the one central, all-sustaining life.

Bahya Ibn Pakuda

The theological treatise of the Spanish-Jewish sage Bahya Ibn Pakuda (c. 1050), who lived in the 11th century, was written in Arabic and known in its Hebrew translation as *Hoboth-Halebaboth* ("Duties of the Heart"); it expresses the rapture of ultimate communion with the Divine, the joys of beholding the beauty of a higher world accessible only to the choice spirits of mankind, in language of rare passion and intensity.

Bahya's mysticism has a twofold foundation. God must be experienced both intellectually and emotionally. But God in His essence is really unknowable. He is "more hidden than anything which is hidden, further away than anything which is far." Hence how can He be known? Only, answers Bahya, by man's reflection upon His greatness and goodness as manifested in the wondrously accurate workings of the natural world. To this end man must go through all the stages of a life of purgation and purification. Guided in this aim by the laws of the Torah and the prescriptions of the rabbis, he will finally reach that pinnacle of faith and love when he will be able to say, as did one of the saints, "Oh! my God thou hast caused me to suffer hunger,

Thou hast left me naked, Thou hast set me down in the
darkness of the night. . .even though Thou burn me
with fire I shall but continue to love Thee and rejoice in
Thee." But Bahya, while favoring a certain measure of
asceticism, felt, like the best mystics of all nations, the
beauteous necessity of man cooperating with his fellow
in all true works of goodness and use.

Judah Ha-Levi

The Spanish-Jewish poet and theologian Judah ha-
Levi (1085-1143) rises to rare heights of mystic perception in his religious poetry as well as in certain portions
of his philosophical treatise, *Kusari*. Spiritual love has
never been more rapturously expressed in the Hebrew
language than in his collected poetry. The wooing of
God by the soul, God as the friend to whom the soul
turns when the hour is darkest, the sense of both the
body's and soul's complete subjection to God—all these
and many kindred outpourings of the mystic are prom-
inent throughout. But the poet had another ideal
besides God. This was the rehabilitation of Zion. Isai-
ah's striking picture of Jerusalem as the bride of God,
as well as the rabbinic-mystic interpretation of "dove,"
"my beloved," "love," and similar words and phrases
in the Song of Songs are the foundations on which the
poet builds up the edifice of his mystic vision concerning the new Jerusalem and an Israel restored thereto.
In the *Kusari*, the idea is philosophically applied to the
Shekinah ("Divine Presence").[62] It is said that only
Palestine could be the land of prophecy, the land where
the first germs of religion grew, because only there
could the Shekinah exist—the Shekinah which ever

---

[62] *Kusari*, ii, 14-18.

awaits and yearns to become joined with the people who have rendered themselves morally and physically fit to receive the gift.

Moses Hayyim Luzzatto

The poet and theologian Moses Hayyim Luzzatto (born at Padua 1707, died 1747) claimed to have received divine revelations from a heavenly genius, and his numerous mystical works written in Hebrew and Aramaic—in some of which he imitated the language of the *Zohar*—fell under the ban of the religious leaders of his day. His ethical treatise *Mesilath Y'sharim* ("Path of the Upright") is based on a saying of a famous miracle-working Rabbi of the 2nd century A.D., Phinechas ben Yair. It details the steps by which man renders himself worthy to receive the Holy Spirit. To follow the full spiritual content of the Law is, to Luzzatto, the goal of him who is at once gifted with wisdom and fear of God. The road lies through "carefulness," "diligence," "cleanliness," "abstemiousness," "purity," "piety," "humility," "fear of sin," and "holiness." The result is the incoming of the Holy Spirit.

Hasidism an Offshoot of the Kabbala

Hasidism ("Pietism") may be considered to be a child of the Kabbala. While the Kabbala was limited to a select few who could fathom its doctrines and interpret them in necessary instances, Hasidism consisted of teachings derived from the Kabbala and directed to the masses, the simple folk, who could understand and appreciate them.

The innovator of the Hasidic movement was known as Israel, but by virtue of the love and respect he received from his followers he was given the appellation Ba-al Shem Tov ("Master of the Good Name").

The Ba-al Shem Tov was born in 1700 in Okup on the border of Volhynia and Podolia, and spent more of his childhood in the solitude of the woods than with other children. He grew up to be a person of great sensitivity, which manifested itself by his concern for the ignorant, disturbed brethren not only of his area, but wherever they might be. Aside from this noble human quality, he was engrossed in thoughts about God and the universe which were inspired by his study of the *Zohar,* and his study of the Kabbala.

At one point in his life, he felt called upon to lead his people in their spiritual life. The teachings he brought to them, the movement he established, was given the name of Hasidism.

The importance of the Ba-al Shem, even though he contributed little to Jewish mystical thought, lay in the fact that he introduced a new application of mysticism to life and conduct. The new way of life was chiefly distinguished by its demonstrative piety. For this reason, no doubt, his followers adopted the name of Hasidim or "pietists."

In Hasidism, the tendency to permeate the whole of the religious life with mystical elements reached its fullest development.

Central in importance in the teaching of Hasidism was the call for cultivating a feeling of profound rejoicing in God. It is the duty of man to serve God with every one of his movements, Hasidism taught.

The body of man, according to Hasidism, is only an outer robe; his essence lies in the world of thought, in which it is his task to release the hidden "sparks"—

that is, to bring them back to their pure source. The most holy action of man is that of prayer, the main concern of which is not the individual need but the exile and deliverance of the Shekinah (the "Divine Presence"). The pious of the generation, Hasidism stressed, are the soul of the people and of the age.

With the passing of the Ba-al Shem in 1760, others carried on his work and his teachings. However, with each new leader the fire of the movement, the enthusiasm which the Ba-al Shem injected into it, waned. Of course, what really caused Hasidism's decline was that the economic, political, and social conditions which were responsible for its rise radically changed.

In our day, especially in the United States, there are still some individuals who are adherents of the teachings of Hasidism and try to live a Hasidic type of life. But what is truly left of the movement is graphically summed up by the Hebrew novelist and storyteller S.J. Agnon, whose words are quoted by Gershom Scholem:

> When the Ba-al Shem had a difficult task before him, he would go to a certain place in the woods, light a fire, and meditate in prayer—and what he had set out to perform was done. When a generation later the "Maggid" [preacher] of Meseritz was faced with the same task, he would go to the same place in the woods and say: "We can no longer light the fire, but we can still speak the prayers," and what he wanted done became a reality. Again a generation later, Rabbi Moshe Leib of Sassov had to perform this task. And he too went into the woods and said: "We can no longer light a fire, nor do we know the secret meditations belonging to the prayer, but we do know the place in the woods to which it all belongs—and that must be sufficient"; and sufficient it was. But when another generation had passed and Rabbi Israel of Rishin was called upon to perform

the task, he sat down on his golden chair in his castle
and said: "We cannot light the fire, we cannot speak the
prayers, we do not know the place, but we can tell the
story of how it was done."[63]

The Effect of the Kabbala on Jewish Life

The Kabbala in many instances had an ennobling
and purifying effect upon the hearts and minds of the
Jewish people. It portrayed the world as being quintes-
sentially spiritual; it taught a doctrine of an unbroken
intercourse between God and the world; it made the
approach to the Divine easier by making holy living
instead of the intellect the criterion of religion. Nowhere
is the soul spoken of with such ecstasy as in Kabbal-
ism, which holds nothing as material but everything
as ablaze with soul. In distress and darkness, when his
faith and confidence would almost desert him, the Jew
found in the Kabbala hope and promise which enabled
him to pick up his burden and carry on.

Christian Interest in the Kabbala

The first Christian scholar who was attracted to the
Kabbala was Raymond Lulli (born about 1225, died
June 30, 1315). He was called *doctor illuminatus* on
account of his great learning. The Kabbala furnished
him with material for his *Ars Magna*, by which he
thought to bring about an entire revolution in the
methods of scientific investigation, his means being
none other than to letter and number mysticism in its

---

[63] Gershom Scholem, *Major Trends in Jewish Mysticism* (Jerusalem: Schocken Publishing House, 1941), p. 345.

different varieties. But it was Pico della Mirandola (1463-94) who introduced the Kabbala into the Christian world. He considered the Kabbala as the sum of those revealed doctrines of the Jews which were not originally written down but were transmitted by oral tradition. At the insistence of Ezra they were written down during his time so that they might not be lost. Pico maintained that the Kabbala contains all the doctrines of Christianity. He therefore made full use of Kabbalistic ideas in his philosophy, or rather, his philosophy consists of Neoplatonic-Kabbalistic doctrines in Christian garb.

Through Johann Reuchlin (1455-1522) the Kabbala became an important factor in leavening the religious movements at the time of the Reformation.

The increased aversion to scholasticism, especially in the German countries, found a positive support in the Kabbala, for those that were hostile to scholasticism could confront it with another system. Mysticism also hoped to confirm its position by means of the Kabbala and to leave the limits to which it had been confined by ecclesiastical dogma.

Reuchlin, the first important representative of this movement in Germany, distinguished between Kabbalistic doctrines, Kabbalistic art, and Kabbalistic perception. Its central doctrine for him was the Messianology, around which all its other doctrines grouped themselves. And as the Kabbalistic doctrine originated in divine revelation, so was Kabbalistic art derived immediately from divine illumination. By means of this illumination man can gain insight into the contents of Kabbalistic doctrine through the symbolic interpretation of the letters, words, and contents of Scripture; hence the Kabbala is symbolical theology. Whoever would become an adept in the Kabbalistic art, and thereby penetrate Kabbalistic secrets, must have divine illumination and inspiration. The Kabbalist must therefore first of all purify his soul from sin, and then order his life in accord with the precepts of virtue and morality.

Reuchlin's entire philosophical system—the doctrine of God, cognition, etc.—is completely Kabbalistic, as he freely admits. Reuchlin's contemporary Heinrich Cornelius Agrippa of Nettesheim (1487-1535) holds the same views, with this difference that he pays especial attention to the practical side of the Kabbala, namely magic—which he endeavors to develop and explain. In his chief work, *De Occulta Philosophia* (Paris, 1528), he deals principally with the doctrines of God, the Sefiroth, and the division of the universe into three distinct worlds: (1) that of the elements, (2) the heavenly world, and (3) the intelligible world. These worlds, he holds, are intimately connected with one another, the higher ever influencing the lower, and the latter attracting the influence of the former.

Another Christian scholar whose interest in the Kabbala is worth mentioning is Francesco Zorzi (1460-1540). His theosophy is wholly Kabbalistic. His doctrine of the threefold soul is especially characteristic, as he even used the Hebrew terms *Nefesh*, *Ruah*, and *Neshamah*.

Protestant Doctrines and the Kabbala

Natural science of the Reformation period, not yet having attained independence and having been bound up more or less with purely speculative principles, sought support in the Kabbala, which enjoyed a great reputation.

Many conceptions derived from the Kabbala may be found in the doctrines of Protestantism as taught by its first representatives, Martin Luther (1483-1546) and Philip Melanchthon (1497-1560). This is still more the case with the German mystics Valentin Veigel (1533-88) and Jacob Boehme (1575-1624).

In addition to these Christian thinkers who took up the doctrines of the Kabbala and essayed to work them over in their own way, Joseph de Voisin (1610-85), Athanasium Kircher (1602-84), and Knorr Baron von Rosenroth endeavored to spread the Kabbala among the Christians by translating Kabbalistic works, which they regarded as most ancient wisdom. Most of them also entertained the belief that the Kabbala contained proofs of the truth of Christianity.

Chapter Five

Christian Mysticism

Mysticism is religion in its purest form.
S.U.

Greek Influence on Christian Mysticism

hristian mysticism points to Plato (c.428-
c.347 B.C.) for its earliest influence. While
there are no biographical incidents indi-
cating that Plato experienced definite
moments of invasion when he felt immediate contacts with the world of higher
reality, his *Dialogues* are pervaded with an invincible
certainty of that world.

There can be little doubt that to Plato more than any
other philosopher we owe the conviction that man's

soul is allied with a realm of Eternal Reality; and that it may be taken as certain that Plato's ultimate position rested on flashes of insight, rather than upon reasoned arguments.

Plato's answer to the question "What is reality?" is that fundamentally it is the forms of things that are real and not matter or "stuff." Things as we perceive them are forever changing and altering. The same thing at different times has different properties. It appears large in some circumstances, and small in others. When we examine the world in terms of what we perceive, we find that it possesses no permanence, stability, or coherence. Such a world cannot be real, but can only consist of illusory appearance.

In the sense world, we discover the first glimmerings of what reality actually is. The forms of things, unlike the things themselves, are unchanging and intelligible. The former are apprehended by reason, the latter by the senses. Individual dogs may be in a continual state of change, but the form of a dog, dogness, is immutable. The meaning of the term "dog" is always the same, even though each particular dog passes through an ever-changing life cycle. Hence Plato contended that what is real is the totality of forms.

Reality is, then, solely to be identified with Platonic Ideas. These are unaffected by the process of change in the sense world. To the question "Why do the Ideas have the characteristics they do?" Plato offered a somewhat mysterious and mystical answer. All the Ideas share in common the features of permanence and intelligibility. To account for this, Plato proposed that there must be an Idea of Ideas, the Idea of the Good, which is the ultimate reality and the source of the reality of everything else.

Plato likened the Idea of the Good to the sun, which

illuminates everything including itself. When one has the experience of knowing the Idea of the Good, suddenly "everything is clear." The awareness of this Idea is like a mystical experience. It is beyond understanding. It is ineffable. And yet it explains all else. When one has had this experience, one then comprehends why all the other Ideas are what they are, because they partake of or participate in the Idea of the Good.

Plato's metaphysical theory tries to give some account of the world of appearance and proposes an answer to the question "What is Reality?" But it also leads to some conclusion about man's relation to the real world.

A human being belongs to both the real and the apparent world. His body is physical; consequently he is part of the visible, material world. His sense information consists of the images he receives of the apparent, illusory world. On the other hand, his mind is immaterial and is capable of knowing the real world of Platonic Ideas. In addition to possessing a body and a mind, Plato maintained that the human being also has a soul which directs his activities and interests. Man's body wants to descend into the material world of appearance, while his mind wants to soar upward in order to contemplate the real world. The human soul is portrayed as being like the driver of a chariot, directing two horses pulling in opposite directions. The soul is attempting to steer while it is trapped in its prison, the body.

The soul that succeeds in directing a harmonious life under the circumstances just described will eventually lead the human being to liberation from the sense world. This is accomplished by eliminating one's dependence upon the physical world. Even though one lives in physical circumstances, and has physical needs, these do not necessarily have to dominate one's life. A life directed in terms of the ultimate goal of contemplating reality, while lived in a physical context, should, after the death of the body, enable the soul to soar upward to the perfect world of Ideas.

Plato's metaphysical theory led to an other-worldly view which is usually called "Platonism." Many of Plato's followers have emphasized the world of Ideas, while derogating the sense world. His followers have insisted that what is worthwhile in the world can be found only in the Real world. The physical world is of little importance, they have claimed. Man, in their view, should pursue the goal of contemplation, of the world of Ideas, in order to obtain a mystical insight into the nature of ultimate reality.

Next to Plato in his influence on Christian mysticism comes his best interpreter, Plotinus, who was born near Alexandria in 205 A.D. and died in Rome in 270. He was one of the greatest of the philosophers of antiquity and one of the profoundest and most influential mystics of all time. His own account of his transcient experience is taken from the fourth and sixth books of the *Enneads*. "Many times it has happened," he reports, "that I have been lifted out of the body into myself, becoming external to all things and self-centered, beholding a marvelous beauty, more than ever assured of community with the loftiest order, acquiring identity with the divine."[64] Another passage reaches an even greater height when the soul attains its goal: "Once *there* the soul will barter this experience for nothing the universe holds, not though one would make over to her the heavens entire; than this there is nothing higher, nothing more good. Above this there is no passing."[65]

---

[64]   *Enneads*, iv. 8:1
[65]   Ibid., vi. 7:34

Plotinus is in the fullest sense the "Father" of Western mysticism. He made the vision of God and union with Him the goal of life for man. To achieve that goal, according to Plotinus, the soul must forsake, must withdraw from everything external, everything unreal, everything finite, and must concentrate on the immutable, perfect, eternal, absolute Reality.

Plotinus more emphatically than any other philosopher after Plato established the doctrine that the universe in its ultimate nature is spiritual. His explanation of how a material world flowed from a spiritual being not only influenced Christian mysticism but Jewish and Islamic as well.

The gist of his explanation is that, as the light of the sun, without effort on the sun's part and without subtracting from its substance, forever streams from that source, with diminishing power as it is more remote from its source, until it is lost in the darkness, so from the First Principle, which is the First Cause, proceeds the Intelligence (*Nous*), from it the World Soul, and from this in turn Primal Matter and the corporeal universe. This procession is not in space and time, for these emerge only in the last stage. Thus all is from God, and God is in all, yet in such a way that this absolute transcendence is not impaired.

The individual souls, which constitute a system of souls in the World Soul, descending into the bodily world, preoccupied with the things of sense, become unmindful of their divine origin and therewith lose their freedom. From this bondage, which subjects the soul to the round of rebirths, it can be saved only by turning its thought away from the things of sense and upward to Reason (Nous), and through it to the superrational good, to God. This last stage in its reascent can, so long as the soul is in the body, be accomplished

only in an ecstasy, transcending sense, reason, intuition, and consciousness—a supreme moment in which
the soul loses itself in God.

Plotinus made the vision of God and union with Him
the goal of life for man. It is the apex of man's upward
journey. To achieve this end, the soul must come away
from division to unity, from distraction to serenity,
from the many to the One. It must, therefore, arrive
stripped, denuded, emptied. Contemplation, which
means mystical vision, is the utmost, the completest
concentration, from which multiplicity, mutability,
and divisions of time and place are lost in indivisible
unity.[66]

Plotinus, together with a few other Neoplatonists of
his day, set the intellectual pattern for Christian
mysticism.

A person who was deeply influenced by Plotinus'
mysticism, and who in turn imparted much of this
influence to Western Christianity, was St. Augustine
(354-430) of Hippo in Africa.

In the Seventh Book of his *Confessions*, he describes
how his whole intellectual outlook was changed by his
contact with the teaching of Plotinus. He writes: "Thou
O Lord, didst provide me with certain books of the
Platonists [in fact, the Neoplatonists[67]] translated
from the Greek into Latin...."[68] "I began now to see
with the eye of my soul above my mind the Light
unchangeable; I found the unchangeable and true

---

[66]   Rufus Jones, *Studies in Mystical Religion* (London, 1909).

[67]   Neoplatonism is the name of an Alexandrian school of philosophy of which Plotinus was the chief representative. The members
of this school called themselves Neoplatonists. They concerned
themselves with the study of reality, which, according to them, was
the result of emanations at various removes from the One or God.

[68]   *Confessions*, vii. 9.

Eternity of Truth [God] above my changeable mind.
And with the flash of one trembling glance, I arrived at
That Which Is."⁶⁹

Another major transmitter of the mystical contribution of Neoplatonism to Western Christianity wrote
under the name of "Dionysius." His 5th-century writings consist of four books and a collection of ten letters:
On the Celestial Hierarchy; *On the Ecclesiastical Hierarchy*; *On the Divine Names*; *On Mystical Theology*;
and *Epistles*.

"Dionysius" for centuries was thought to be St.
Paul's convert on the Areopagus (hence the common
appellation "Dionysius the Areopagite").

Modern scholars are convinced that the works
attributed to "Dionysius" are actually the efforts of a
Neoplatonist Christian who, following an ancient custom, wrote under a pseudonym.

In any case, the writings of "Dionysius," from the
middle of the 9th century on, became an indispensable
part of the spiritual culture of Europe. His writings
present Neoplatonism after it had undergone some
changes at the hands of the Athenian philosopher
Proclus (410-485).

"Dionysius" took the system of thought as it came
from Proclus and Christianized it. Henceforth, until
the Reformation, all Christian mysticism would bear
his influence.

"Dionysius" thinks of God as utterly transcendent in
terms similar to those used by Plotinus. The universe,
according to his system, has flowed out from God. It is
a divine emanation and there is also a cosmic process
of "return" back to the Eternal One. Between the Godhead and the world in space and time there is a de-

---

⁶⁹   Ibid., vii. 10-17.

scending order of sub-realities, which, according to "Dionysius," are nine "Celestial Hierarchies"— Seraphim, Cherubim, Thrones, Dominations, Virtues, Powers, Principalities, Archangels, and Angels.

For "Dionysius" the transcendency of God means that no predicates, even moral ones, can be attributed to Him. He is an inaccessible Being. He is above all concepts, even that one of "Being." He is beyond the range of thought, knowledge, intellect, or any faculty man possesses. He is hidden, ineffable, incomprehensible, since there is nothing else in the universe *like Him*. The only possible approach, therefore, is the way of negation. "In ascending from below to that which is above," he says, "in proportion to the ascent, the discourse is contracted and, after a complete ascent, it will become wholly voiceless and will become completely united to the unutterable."[70]

The great interpreter of "Dionysius" was Maximus Confessor (d. 662). The purification of the soul, which in "Dionysius" is intellectual, is in Maximus the removal of the moral hindrances to the attainment of perfection, especially the extirpation of the passions. The soul that loves God yields itself wholly to the enfolding divine embrace, enters into ineffable communion with Him, and loses itself in the ocean of the godhead.

The writings of "Dionysius" and Maximus have been crucial to mystics in the West, as well as to mystics in the Eastern church.

Still another individual from the Greek world who made a substantial contribution to Christian mysticism was the Jewish philosopher, allegorist, and mystic Philo Judaeus (20 B.C.—A.D. 50), of Alexandria.

To the question of how God, who is all-perfect, all-

---

[70]   *On Myst. Theol.*, iii. 1

holy, created imperfect man and a world of matter, Philo's answer was *Logoi*, divine agencies which, while being in some senses inherent in God, are, in other ways and various times, exterior to Him, and are responsible for the material things in the universe.

Philo's idea of Logos has played a major role in Christian theology and Christian mysticism. Logos, in the course of time, was interpreted to mean the Son of God—the Word of God.

The most unmystical of the Greek philosophers was Aristotle. Yet he too must be given credit for having contributed, even though indirectly, to Christian mysticism. His contribution came as a result of his interpreting the nature of man's mind. In his interpretation he maintained that the human mind has two *levels* which are wholly unlike. One level he called "passive reason," through which we receive our sense impressions, all our items of information, and the fact-elements of knowledge. It is a part of nature. It has its parallel in the animals and it presents no more mystery than any other feature of life does. "Active Reason," on the other hand, belongs on an entirely different level. It is utterly unique. It cannot be explained in terms of anything else. It could not have come "from outside," from things, from an empirical world. It is the creative power in us by which we organize our facts of experience, attain to universal truths, transcend the finite, and become able to think our own thoughts and live in a supersensuous world of spiritual realities. Active Reason attains its object by a supreme act of vision. Aristotle left the origin of the Active Reason in man unexplained. Aristotle's great commentator, Alexander of Aphrodisias, who flourished about 200 A.D., was the first philosopher to identify explicitly this Active Reason of Aristotle with the *Eternal Nous*, the divine Rea-

son. It is of God, he said, and it operates in God. The
ideas which this higher reason presents to passive
human reason are Divine Ideas—thoughts which God
thinks in us. Plotinus calls Divine Reason the Apex of
the Soul.[71] He says of the Apex of the Soul that "it is so
akin to God that it is one with God and not merely
united to Him."

In considering Aristotle's Active Reason, the eternal
ground of man's inmost self, Pico Della Mirandola, in
the 15th century, said, "it is a commonplace of the
schools that man is a little world [microcosmos] in
which we may discern a body mingled of earthly elements and ethereal breath, and the vegetable life of
plants, and the sense of the lower animals, and reason,
and the intelligence of angels and a *likeness to God*."[72]

Another reason why Aristotle's name figures so
prominently in Christian mysticism, and is also
brought into Jewish and Islamic mysticism, is his
theology. Even though scholars are of the opinion that
he is not the author of what is referred to as *The Theology of Aristotle*, nevertheless it has been absorbed into
the various mystical systems and he is credited with it.
Whoever is the author of *The Theology of Aristotle*
expresses himself as a mystic. He says: "Often I was
alone with my soul. I entered as pure substance into my
real self, turning away from all that is external to what
is within. I became pure knowing at once the knower
and the known. How astonished I was to behold beauty
and splendor in my own self and to recognize that I am
part of the sublime Divine World, endowed even with
creative life! In this discovery of self, I was lifted above
the world of the senses, even above the world of spirits,

[71]   *Enneads*, vi. 9:8.
[72]   Rufus Jones, *The Flowering of Mysticism* (New York: Hafner
Publishing Co., 1971), p. 14.

up to the Divine, where I beheld a Light so beautiful that no tongue can express it nor can ear understand it."[73]

Gnosticism and Christian Mysticism

The word Gnosticism is derived from the Greek word *gnosis*, which means "knowledge."

Gnosticism was a movement of religious syncretism (a fusion of different independent beliefs), which maintained itself side by side with Christianity as the latter was gradually crystallizing into the ancient Catholic church.

The movement first came into prominence in the opening years of the 2nd century; it reached its height in the third quarter of the 3rd century, after which it began to wane. Offshoots of it, however, continued on into the 4th and 5th centuries, and many of its ideas survived among later mystics.

Among the majority of the followers of the movement gnosis was understood not as meaning "knowledge" or understanding in the ordinary sense of the word, but "revelation." The Gnostic sects claimed that they possessed a secret, mysterious type of knowledge that in no way was accessible to those outside their groups, and that their special knowledge was not based on reflection but solely on revelation.

Gnosticism, in all its various actions, its form and character, resembles the mystic religions which were so characteristic of the religious life of the people of antiquity.

As in many mystical religions, so in Gnosticism the ultimate aim is individual salvation, the assurance of a

---

[73] Ibid., p. 36.

fortunate destiny of the soul after death. Gnosticism is dominated by the idea that it is most important for the Gnostic's soul to be able to find its way back through the lower worlds to the kingdom of light, to the supreme deity of heaven, the source of its origin.

The essential part of what we call Gnosticism was already in existence and fully developed before the rise of Christianity. The fundamental ideas of Gnosticism and of early Christianity had a kind of magnetic attraction for each other. What drew these two forces together was the energy exerted by the universal idea of salvation in both systems.

It was no accident that pre-Christian Gnosticism eventually identified itself with Christianity. The earlier stages of its history appear to have been a preparation for it. The Eastern religions were to an extent akin to Christianity in their presuppositions and motives. They represented a striving after purity and redemption and a belief that the true path to blessedness could be discovered only in the light of a Divine revelation.

Gnosticism was above all a religion of sacraments and mysteries. Through its syncretic origin, it introduced for the first time into Christianity a whole mass of sacramental, mystical ideas.

Most Gnostic groups enjoined a strict ascetic discipline on their followers. They condemned bodily gratifications including the use of flesh as food. Their otherworldliness contributed to an atmosphere of religious fervor favorable to mysticism.

Under the influence of Persian traditions, Gnostics attached a great importance to the angelic hierarchies and to their world of mystical light, intermediary between the Transcendent Causeless Cause and the world of concrete forms and bodies.

It seems likely that, because of its considerable extension over all the Greco-Roman empire, and because of the marked otherworldly character of some of its doctrines, Gnosticism was one of the major historical factors which influenced the early development of Christian mysticism.

Asceticism and Christian Mysticism

From the very beginning of Christianity asceticism appears to be one of its common practices. Those who aspired to higher achievements in the Christian life mortified the flesh. Continence was elevated to the first rank among the virtues of the married as well as the unmarried; a meager diet without meat or wine, varied by periods of fasting, was an approved method of subduing the appetites and passions. This self-discipline did not require separation from society or the abandonment of ordinary occupations, the activities of everyday life.

In the 3rd and 4th centuries, in Egypt, a new type of asceticism developed, which spread rapidly through the Christian world. At first the ascetics withdrew from the city to some uninhabited spot nearby to devote themselves undistracted to religious exercises. Soon the desire for more complete seclusion drew some of them deeper into the desert, where they formed a kind of colony, living in simple huts and subjecting themselves to such privations as seemed good in their own eyes. Some of them retreated into still more unhospitable solitudes and would come together for services only on Sundays. This form of monachism prevailed in Lower and Middle Egypt. Its practitioners came to be known as eremites, from which the English word "hermit" is derived. The most famous representative of this type of monachism is Saint Anthony.

About the same time that the eremite form of monachism was introduced, a man named Pachomius, introduced the coenobite type of monachism. The word coenobite refers to "community life." It differed from the eremite type by practicing its asceticism within the community instead of outside of it.

In the year 320 A.D. Pachomius founded a monastery in Upper Egypt. There the life of the monks was ordered by rule; their worship, their work, their food, their fasts, and their dress were minutely prescribed. The monastery was an economic community: whatever it produced beyond its own needs was either sold or exchanged for other goods. This type of monastery, which at first was limited to men, soon became the model for women as well.

In the 4th century, the monastic movement spread from Egypt to Palestine and to Syria. It soon reached Asia Minor, where Basil gave it the form which prevailed in the Greek Church and has continued to this day.

The organizer of Western monachism was Benedict of Nursia. His famous rule for the monks of Monte Cassino (529 A.D.) was based on an avoidance of excess in anything. The organization and discipline of the monastery were completely regulated; the rule enjoined the strictest obedience to the superior. Benedict also founded a corresponding order for nuns. His sister Scholastica was its first abbess. The Benedictine form eventually became the prevalent type of monachism in the Western Church, as that of Basil was in the Eastern Churches.

The service which the Benedictine monasteries rendered to civilization is inestimable. They kept the lamp of learning burning through the Dark Ages. In their libraries was preserved what we possess of the heritage of ancient Rome and of early Christian literature in Latin.

Since monachism represented the higher Christian life, priests and bishops were chosen from among the monks with increasing frequency. This strengthened the feeling that all clergy should lead an ascetic life after the monastic pattern. Clerical celibacy was an ideal which sought to convert itself into a rule, especially in the West. Ambrose, Augustine, and Jerome were advocates of it; popes and synods enacted it into the law of the Church.

The primary aim of asceticism was the subjugation of the flesh in order to attain the mystical experience of union with God.

The Effect of Scholastic Theology on Christian Mysticism

There was a stirring of intellectual life in Europe in the 11th century. It manifested itself in a quickened interest in theological questions and the introduction of new methods in the treatment of them. It was in this age that the first universities began to grow out of the cathedral schools and supersede them. The transition was so gradual that exact dates for it are arbitrary.

In the universities Scholastic theology, which is the greatest achievement of the 12th and 13th centuries, was developed. The doctrines of the Church were now submitted to logical scrutiny.

The first attempt to construct a complete system of theology in the light of the new learning was the *Summa Universae Theologiae* of Alexander of Hales (d. 1245), and his example was followed by others. On the question of the relation of philosophy to theology, he held that philosophical problems are to be treated as such and not confused with speculative theology. On the other hand, he was convinced that, though philosophy may demonstrate the existence and attributes of God and His relation to the universe, specifically Christian doctrines such as the Trinity and the Incarnation are beyond its field.

Thomas Aquinas (1225-1274), whose *Summa Theologica* was regarded as the supreme achievement of Scholastic theology, considered theology as a science which brings into an organic and rational whole the knowledge of God which is attainable by reason and that which is above reason but not contrary to reason is given by revelation. It is not a practical but a theoretical science; knowledge of God is an end, not a means.

Johannes Duns Scotus (d. 1308) set narrower limits to the competence of reason than Aquinas; not only the superrational doctrines of the Trinity and the Incarnation, but the life of God, His reason, His will, foreknowledge and foreordination, the immortality of the human soul, and divine judgment are not susceptible to demonstration in a strict sense. Theology rests on the authority of Scripture and the Church, and the only certainty is that of faith.

In the 14th century, Occam (d. 1349), a pupil of Duns Scotus, came forth with a theory called "Nominalism." This theory led him to deny the possibility of attaining certainty by the rational processes in which his predecessors had such confidence. Not only can the truths of religion, Scotus argued, not be demonstrated by reason, they cannot even be proved to be rational—rather the contrary. They are to be apprehended solely by faith, on the authority of revelation; and if God in His inscrutable wisdom had ordered that the opposite should be true and right (for example, that pure selfishness should be meritorious), it would have been so reason notwithstanding.

The rise of universities in the 11th century, and the

development of a theology based on reason in the 12th century resulted in an intensification of interest in mysticism. Outstanding representatives of mystical thought of this period are Bernard of Clairvaux and Hugh of St. Victor. Turning against the theologians who reduced the mysteries of the Christian religion to a shallow reasonableness, Bernard and Hugh maintained that there is a knowing which is beyond the discursive intelligence, that there are truths that are above reason. Such truths are to be accepted by faith on the authority of Scripture and the Church; only by the mystical vision, or intuition, is it possible for faith to be transformed into knowledge. The soul rises to the height of immediate knowledge by three stages: *cogitatio, meditatio, contemplatio*; the last alone can give an invincible conviction of those objects of faith which are above reason.

The mystics of the medieval period were not content to keep the secrets of their mystical knowledge to themselves or reveal it to a few special souls. They preached it and wrote about it as a way of life for the laity as well as the clergy. This popularization brought home to the listeners and readers the important lesson that religion is essentially an inner life having its expression and criterion in Christian conduct, and not merely the acceptance of the dogmas and doctrines of the Church.

Hildegarde of Bingen

Germany gave rise to a host of mystics in the 12th, 13th, and 14th centuries. A number of these were women.

Christian mysticism in Germany began with Hildegarde of Bingen (1098-1179). She possessed an extraordinary intellect and powerful imagination. In a letter which St. Bernard of Clairvaux addressed to her, he remarked, "You are said to be so favored that the hidden things of heaven are revealed to you and it is reported that the Holy Spirit makes known to you those things which pass man's understanding. Wherefore I entreat and humbly pray that you would make remembrance of me before God and of those who are joined with me in spiritual society. I trust that when you are united to God in the Spirit you will be able to help and profit us much."[74]

The most significant current of thought which she set in motion and which long continued to influence the medieval mind was her theory of cosmic vitalism. Her view of the universe was the outcome of "visions" of an unusual type. "These visions which I saw," she says, "I beheld neither in sleep, nor in dream, nor in madness, nor with my carnal eyes, nor with the ears of the flesh, nor in hidden places, but wakeful alert, with the eyes of the spirit and with inward ears, I perceived them in open view and according to the will of God. And how this was compassed is hard indeed for human flesh to search out."[75]

The following is a description of one of her experiences: "From my infancy up to the present time, I now being more than seventy years of age, I have always seen this light [a blinding, glittering light, the color of flame, red as fire] in my spirit and not with external eyes, nor with any thoughts of my heart nor with help from my senses. But my outward eyes remain open and the other corporeal senses retain their activity. The light which I see is not located but yet is more brilliant

[74] *Life and Works of St. Bernard*, ed. Don John Mabillon, trans. S.J. Earles, Vol. II, pp. 915-917.

[75] Charles Singer, *Magic to Science* (New York, 1928), p. 231.

than the sun, nor can I examine its height, length, or breadth, and I name it 'the cloud of the living light.' And as sun, moon, and stars are reflected in water, so the writings, sayings, virtues, and works of men shine in it before me, and whatever I thus see in vision the memory thereof remains long with me. Likewise I see, hear, and understand almost in a moment and I set down what I thus learn. But sometimes I behold within this light another light which I name 'the living Light itself.' And when I look upon it every sadness and pain vanishes from my memory, so that I am again as a simple maid and not as an old woman."[76]

Mechthilde of Magdeburg

The life of Mechthilde of Magdeburg (1207-1282) is presented by her in her book *Life and Revelations.* In it she speaks of her visions, ecstasies, illuminations, and miraculous experiences. She talks much of mystical marriage, of mystical union. Her ecstasies were times of intense concentration during which she appears to have fused together the mystical ideas which she had accumulated from her reading and conversations and to have felt these ideas come before her mind as revelations.

Some scholars are of the opinion that Mechthilde of Magdeburg is the Matilda of Dante's vision. "There appeared to me (even as appears suddenly something doth turn aside through every wonder every other thought) a lady all alone, who went along singing and culling floweret after floweret."[77] Canto xxxiii, line 119 of the *Purgatorio* tells the reader that this "singing

76   Ibid., pp. 232-233.
77   *Purgatorio*, xxviii. 37-41.

lady" who represents the active life is Matilda. Commentators have usually assumed that she was Countess Matilda of Tuscany, and that Dante could not have known the story of Mechthilde of Magdeburg.

Mechthilde represents one of the most striking and most characteristic of the German women mystics.

Meister Eckhart

One of the greatest Christian mystics was Meister Eckhart (1260-1327). He was born in Hochheim, Germany. At about the age of forty he pursued advanced studies at the University of Paris. There he acquired the degree of Meister, probably in 1303.

Few men have ever had an opinion of the soul such as he had. "So like Himself God made man's soul that nothing else on earth or in heaven resembles God so closely as does the human soul."[78] The Ground of man's soul is an external reality. It is beyond and above time. "The loftiest part of the soul stands above time and knows nothing of time."[79]

"Clearing the way through the senses we rise past our own mind to the wisdom of God. We feel an inkling of the perfection and stability of eternity, for there is neither time nor space, neither before nor after, but everything present in one new, fresh, springing *now*, where millenniums last no longer than the twinkling of an eye."[80]

"There is," he says, "a principle in the soul untouched by time and flesh, flowing from Spirit, remaining in the

---

[78]   Meister Eckhart, *Sermons*, trans. C. de B. Evans (London, 1924), vi. p. 2-8.

[79]   Ibid., xi. p. 41.

[80]   Ibid., xii. p. 47.

Spirit, itself altogether spiritual. In this principle is
God, ever verdant, flowering in all the joy and glory of
His actual self.... Sometimes I have called this principle
the tabernacle of the soul, sometimes a spiritual Light,
anon I say it is a Spark. But now I say that it is somewhat more exalted over this and that than the heavens
are above the earth. So now I name it in a nobler
fashion than before as regarding rank and mode which
it transcends. It is free of all names, it is void of all
forms. It is one and simple, as God is one and simple,
and no man can in any wise behold it."[81]

Eckhart's mystical doctrine of the Ground of the soul
is, probably, the best approach for understanding, or at
least for glimpsing, his profound doctrine of the Godhead as the Ground, the Source, the Fount of all that we
mean by the Divine, by God as expressed or revealed.

Concerning God, Eckhart says, "Many persons
imagine that there is 'creaturely being' *here* and
'divine being' yonder. That is not so. A man beholds
God in this life in the same perfection and is blessed in
exactly the same way as in the after-life." Eckhart is
confident that there can be a *birth* into all the fullness
of the life of God here and now.

"God expects one thing of you," he says, "and that is
that you should come out of yourself insofar as you are
a created being and let God be God in you." There is a
possible *union* which is beyond the framework of space
and time where the eternal birth brings the soul into
the joy and peace and freedom of the divine life—real
life, life at its deepest.

The full significance of Eckhart is not fully felt until
one sees in him a guide of life who reaches a depth of
unity which transcends the dualism of both subject

---

[81]   Ibid., viii. pp. 36-37.

and object and the natural and the supernatural. For
him the essentially divine reality is not external to the
soul, but is actually experienced inwardly.

Johannes Tauler

Johannes Tauler (1300-1361) is known as the great
preacher of Strasbourg, Germany. He lacked the education of Eckhart, but the people who flocked to hear
his sermons felt that he was one of them, that he understood them, suffered with them, and shared their sorrows as well as their joys and hopes. He did not depend
upon books for his sermons. He spoke out of his heart,
out of his soul.

Tauler was very much in tune with the people of his
day who aspired to union with God and a life of the
spirit; they mourned over the corruptions that they saw
and felt in the Church which they loved.

Tauler, as Eckhart did, held that there is a divine
Ground in the human soul through which there can be
a *birth* into a newness of life and a direct partaking of
Eternity. The spiritual goal of life is the attainment of
union with God in the center of man's being, in the
unseen depths of the spirit where he sinks himself into
the Divine Abyss. When God finds a person thus
simply and nakedly turned toward Him, He bends
down into the depths of the pure soul and draws him up
into His own uncreated essence, so that the spirit
becomes one with Him.[82]

Tauler is very insistent that everything of "the creature," everything which belongs in the sphere of

---

[82]   Sermon for the fifteenth Sunday after Trinity.

"nature," must be laid low, reduced to absolute nothingness. We must be "like a man who has a dart in his body which he cannot pull out without giving himself pain, and who if he does not pull it out will have to suffer still greater pain."[83]

Utter humility is one of the first steps on the highway of holiness. The soul must sink down into absolute seclusion to become "lost" that it may be "found." The fearless knight and dearest friend of God must learn how to "drink the cup of the Lord" and submit to suffering, even to a dying life.[84]

On the subject of love he says, "A love which costs nothing is worthless." It is an inner, living love which brings the soul back to its true Source and into union with God, who Himself *is* love. "It is just as impossible for a man to possess God without love as it is impossible that a man can exist without a soul.... So long as thou hast a whole and undivided love toward all men, a share of the virtues and divine influences which God intends to bestow on men will flow out through thee in this love of thine. The moment thou severest thyself from this spirit of universal love thou wilt miss this outflow of divine love which otherwise would fill thy vessel overbrimming full."[85]

The test of a mystical experience, Tauler told his listeners, is not its emotional upheaval, but its effect on action and on the moral life—the power to endure suffering and to exhibit love and sympathy. "No virtue is to be trusted until it has been put into action."

Tauler's one ambition was to be a devoted "Friend of God" through inward fellowship with Him.

---

[83] Sermon on the Feast of St. Laurence.
[84] Sermon on the Feast of Martyrs.
[85] Sermon for the fourth Sunday after Trinity.

Heinrich Suso

Heinrich Suso was born in Constance, Germany, in 1295 and died in the year 1365. He possessed a rare mind and a high quality of intellectual and poetic power. At the age of eighteen, he dedicated his life to God. He made up his mind once and for all that his refractory body was to be disciplined. His inner voice told him that "the man who tries to hold by the tail that slippery fish, the eel, and to begin a holy life luke-warmly will be deceived in both cases."[86]

At the time of his decision, Suso had his first ecstatic experience. He speaks of his experience in the third person. "His soul was caught up in ecstasy, whether in the body or out of the body, and he saw and heard what no tongue could tell. It was without form or mode, and yet it contained within itself the entrancing delight-fulness of all forms and modes. His heart was athirst, yet satisfied, his mind was joyous and blooming; wishes were stilled in him and desires had departed. He did but gaze fixedly on the dazzling effulgence, in which he found oblivion of himself and all things. Was it day or night? He knew not. It was a breaking forth of the sweetness of eternal life, felt as present in the still-ness of unvarying contemplation.... This overpowering rapture lasted about an hour and a half. When he came to himself he was altogether like a man who has come from another world."[87]

Suso's *Autobiography* and his *Book of Heavenly Wisdom* give a vivid picture of his spiritual life, with his whole being set on fire with love for the wisdom that he felt was granted to him.

---

[86] *Autobiog.*, p. 8.
[87] Ibid., pp. 9-10.

Suso believed that he possessed the power to *see* what was going on in his heart. On one occasion he reports that the flesh covering his heart became transparent and he saw Eternal Wisdom in lovely form sitting tranquilly beside his own soul and both encircled in the arms of God.[88]

Suso surpasses all the great mystics of his period in the excess of his self-inflicted sufferings and also in the frequency of his ecstasies.

Suso had many disciples, many followers, especially in the convents for women.

Despite Suso's insistence upon withdrawal from objects of sense and his glorification of abstraction, he was too much of a poet not to appreciate the beautiful things in God's visible world.

A few passages from his writings are worthwhile remembering: "There is nothing more painful than suffering, and nothing more joyful than to have suffered."[89] "He who is interior amid exterior things is much more interior than he who is only interior within himself."[90]

"Be steadfast and never rest content until thou hast obtained the Now of Eternity as the present possession in this life."[91]

Jan Ruysbroeck

Jan Ruysbroeck is the greatest Flemish mystic. He was born in the village of Ruysbroeck not far from the

---

[88] Ibid., p. 22.
[89] *External Wisdom*, p. 75.
[90] *Autobiog.*, p. 218.
[91] Ibid., p. 222.

city of Brussels in 1293. He was ordained as a priest at
the age of twenty-four.

Ruysbroeck's life has two stages to it. The first stage
covers his life as a priest in Brussels. The second stage
covers the mystical aspect of his life.

The most significant event in the life of Ruysbroeck
was his decision to turn from his life as priest to the life
of a hermit. One of the reasons for his decision was his
disturbing impression of the worldliness of the Church.

At the age of fifty he retreated to a forest called the
Green Vale. There he prayed, meditated, pondered,
purified his life. There he wrote many books which
reflect his deepest self.

The titles of his books are: *The Book of the Kingdom
of God's Lovers*; *The Book of the Spiritual Tabernacle*;
The Adornment of the Spiritual Marriage; *The Book of
the Sparkling Stone*; *The Book of the Supreme Truth*;
The Mirror of Eternal Salvation; *The Seven Degrees of
Love*; *The Seven Cloisters*; *The Twelve Points of True
Faith*; *The Book of the Four Temptations and the
Twelve Beguines*.

In his book *The Supreme Truth*, as well as in his
other writings, Ruysbroeck tries to make clear the distinction between God and the highest created being. It
is a deep error, he maintains, to say that persons shall
be so absorbed with God in Essential Blessedness that
nothing shall remain apart.[92]

In another passage of the same book he writes: "As
air is penetrated by the brightness and heat of the sun,
and iron is penetrated by fire, so that it works through
fire the works of fire, since it burns and shines like the
fire. . .yet each of these keeps its own nature—the fire
does not become iron, and the iron does not become fire,

---

[92]   *The Book of Supreme Truth*, chap. iv.

for the iron is within the fire and the fire is within the iron, so likewise God is in the being of the soul. The creature never becomes God as God never becomes creature."[93]

Ruysbroeck is one of the greatest exponents of love among the long list of mystics. This man who never loved a maid and who knew little of romantic love, speaks with rare insight of the intrinsic nature of love. He tells his Beguine women that "love is the way," that they must have "a burning earnestness of love," "a fiery flame of devotion," "a loving longing, leaping of the soul." "Let us love the fathomless love that has loved us from Eternity"—"a tempest of love." "There is nothing in the world that can compare with love."[94]

The life of Ruysbroeck nurtured many a hungry soul. The books which he wrote have silently been working for the past five hundred years penetrating numerous lives and lifting them to higher levels of spirituality. He died in 1391.

Gerard Groote

Gerard Groote was born in 1340 in the town of Deventer, which is on the Yssel, a branch of the great Rhine Basin. He studied in Paris, Prague, and Cologne. He became one of the foremost scholars of his time.

His life was directed by an event at a public game one day in Cologne. A man came quietly to his side and gently said to him, "Why art thou here? Thou ought to become another man." "Another man" Gerard determined to become. His soul after that incident was set on

[93] Ibid., chap. viii.
[94] The passages are from *The Twelve Beguines*.

fire by the spirit of God. He decided that he could best express his true self by sharing his inner feelings about God with others by preaching to them. The effect of his preaching was astonishing. He called his hearers to change their lives as he did his.

Gerard's powerful message, the fearless words by which he revealed the condition to which the Church had fallen, soon aroused the hostility of men of place and influence. An outcry was raised against him and his license to preach was revoked.

In his distressed condition, he heard within his soul the voice of Christ saying to him, "My son, allow not thyself to be discouraged in the labor which thou hast undertaken for my sake, nor be cast down by tribulation; let my promise strengthen and console thee under all circumstances."

Whereupon he offered a prayer of committal that breathes complete resignation: "O loving Father, I deliver into Thy hands myself and all that I am. O Lord, grant me to know what I ought to know, to love what I ought to love, to praise what ought to be praised, to esteem what is precious to Thee, and to abhor what is filthy in Thy sight. Thou knowest what is profitable for my progress; and *how well tribulation* serves to *scour off* the rust *of my defects*" (from his *Diary*).

On the subject of love, he says, "Love is the greatest thing: it makes light what otherwise is heavy; it bears every wrong with serenity. Love carries a burden without feeling its weight. It makes the bitter sweet. There is neither in Heaven nor on earth anything sweeter than love, nothing stronger, nothing loftier, nothing happier, nothing more precious; for love is born of God and cannot rest except in God. Love runs, flies, is happy and free, is held back by nothing. Love knows no measure, feels no burden, considers nothing impossible, is never weary. It is a living flame. *He who is not ready to suffer all things and to be conformed to the will of the Beloved* is not worthy to be called a lover."[95]

Gerard learned in the hard school of life that there is no victory without a fight, no crown of patience without a struggle, and that if one refused to suffer, he also refused to be crowned. All these feelings are recorded in a book he wrote titled *The Spiritual Diary of Gerard Groote.*

Gerard's diary throbs with the depth of human life. It presents a picture of a human soul fighting a real battle with significant issues of life in a world of men and things.

"Thou ought to become *another* man" was the message that transformed him; it served as a ladder for his soul's climb towards higher and higher levels of humanity and work.

The mysticism of Gerard was of the type that brings enlarged life, widened sympathies, an expanded inner depth, rather than moments of ecstatic thrills. He died in the year 1384.

Rulman Merswin and the Friends of God

In the year 1346 an immensely wealthy Strasbourg banker by the name of Rulman Merswin (1307-82) became disenchanted with his material success and decided to dedicate himself to religion. He resolved to devote his wealth to the furtherance of the ever-growing "Friends of God" movement of the period.[96]

---

[95] *The Spiritual Diary of Gerard*, trans. Joseph Malaise, S.J. (New York, 1937).

[96] Anna Groh Seesholtz., *The Friends of God: Practical Mystics of the Fourteenth Century* (New York: A.M., 1934). "The Friends of God" was an informal fellowship of German mystics, in large part laymen, of the 14th century centering around John Tauler and Heinrich Suso.

On St. Martin's Day, November 11, 1347, Merswin experienced his first ecstasy—which greatly strengthened him in his decision. While he was walking in his garden toward evening, reflecting on the false and deceitful joys of the world, he felt spring up within him a profound repentance for his past life and a deep regret that his will had been left free to go wrong. At that instant a radiant light enveloped him. He experienced the sensation of levitation into the air and of being carried around in his garden.[97] When the rapture had passed, he felt inexpressible joy and was invaded by spiritual forces which he had never known before. His conversion began with this striking ecstatic experience. For the next four years he experienced inward struggles and sufferings until his "conversion" was complete.

The early stage of his "new life" was marked by the practice of extreme asceticism. He attacked his body as a hateful object. When John Tauler, Merswin's confessor, learned of his conduct, he urged him to desist from torturing himself.

It was not until Merswin's body was so swollen that he could not move that he then heard a voice saying, "Rulman, rise up and let thy heart rejoice." Immediately he arose, and all his suffering and pain left him.

It was at this point that he felt commanded by the Spirit to write *The Book of the Banner of Christ* and *The Book of the Nine Rocks*.

---

[97] The sense of levitation is a common mystical experience. It does not mean, of course, that the person is actually raised into the air.

Merswin's Banner Book

The Banner Book is addressed to persons who are entering upon the spiritual life.

It is not enough, the book declares, to experience religious transports or to dream of ecstasies of incomparable happiness or to have heavenly visions. No, the true path is through the depths of spiritual poverty, where God touches *the superior forces of the soul.* The hope of Christianity rests on the few, true "Friends of God." Such persons are prepared for their mission by *absolute renunciation of their own will,* by stern refusal to follow the impulses of their own nature and the complete abandonment of themselves to God without reserve or backward look whether God gives them the gift of his grace or withholds it. Finally, they must submit in all humility to the guidance of a mature Friend of God whose superior forces have been enlightened by divine light.

The person who receives here below a single drop from the living fountain which eternally flows in hearts full of love is at once enlightened in the "higher forces of the soul." Henceforth every created thing on earth becomes as nothing compared with God.

The book ends with a description of how Merswin was commanded by God to write it; that God chose him as an instrument of His work.[98]

Merswin's *Book of the Nine Rocks*

The Book of the Nine Rocks is partly ascribed to Merswin and partly to an anonymous author. The

---

[98] The text is printed in full as Appendix II to August Jundt's *Les Amis de Dieu* (Paris, 1879), pp. 393-402.

early part of the book, believed to have been written by
Merswin, consists of a long complaint on the deca-
dence of Christianity. But, through the efforts of the
"Friends of God," the author declares that the corrup-
tion of the Church leadership from the pope down will
eventually be eliminated and Christianity purified.

The part of the book dealing with the Nine Rocks
describes a high, nine-level mountain. On each level
there are Christians wishing to reach the highest form
of spirituality. Some of the climbers do not get beyond
the first level. By virtue of will, some reach higher
levels. But only three reach the top. They are, according to the author, genuine examples of true Christians.
All personal desire is extinct in them. They love all
human beings with an equal love. All fear is banished
from their minds and hearts. Few as they are in
number, the destiny of Christianity rests on them. If
they failed, Christianity would fail along with them.
The few Christians the author has in mind as the pre-
servers of Christianity are the "Friends of God."

Due to the genuineness of the "Friends of God," living on the highest spiritual level, the author contends,
neither pope nor priest is essential to the existence of
Christianity. Only individuals who live their life in
God are essential. Everything outward in the form of
organization of the Church might go, but there can be
no Church without purified, holy lives.

The lesson the author aims to impart through *The
Book of the Nine Rocks* is that it is always the few who
are prepared to sacrifice for the good of the many; that
it is the few who are responsible for the preservation of
that which is worthwhile; that it is the few who are our
models of courage, hope, and love. In relation to Christianity, it is the "Friends of God," though few in

number, upon whom Christianity depends for its rescue from its low state.

Friends of God and *Theologia Germanica*

A characteristic of the mystics of the 14th century is the desire to be anonymous, to hide their identity under a pseudonym. There was a notable sense of humility, a shrinking from any claim of merit or glory, on the part of the mystics, who were eager to be "Friends of God" but who were satisfied to be nameless in the lists of fame. The gem of mystical literature of the period is a little book called *Theologia Germanica*.

The book was probably written in Frankfurt about the year 1350 by a priest of the Teutonic Order. It represents one of the most successful of many attempts to make mystic principles available for the common man. The writing treats briefly of God's truth in the individual soul, of growth toward perfection, of the "Middle Way" between the active and contemplative self. The ideas resemble the teachings of the "Friends of God."

The book was first published in part in 1516 and completed in 1518 by Martin Luther, who gave it its title.[99]

Saint Theresa

Two of the greatest mystics and writers on mysti-

---

[99] Maria David Windstosser, *Etude sur la Theologie Germanique* (Paris, 1911).

cism arose in Spain in the 16th century. These were St.
Theresa (1515-1582) and St. John of the Cross, a
Carmelite.[100]

Theresa's writings are the most complete and vivid
descriptions ever penned on the inner experience of a
saint. Their value as testimony can hardly be exagger-
ated. They contain much excellent counsel.

In her earliest work, *Life*, she distinguishes the
degrees of prayer according to their psychological
effects: the first is meditation, in which all the powers
of the soul act naturally and freely. They work hard
with small results.[101] The second includes recollection
and the "prayer of quiet" wherein the will is united to
God, while the imagination and intellect remain free to
help or hinder this delightful union.[102] In the third
degree these powers are also drawn into union without
either being lost or yet able to tell how they work; this
causes an inebriation, a glorious folly, and leaves
behind it greater effects than quietude.[103] The fourth
state is a complete union of all powers so that it is

---

[100]   The historical origin of the Carmelites is placed at the middle
of the 12th century, when a crusader from Calabria named Birthold
and ten companions established themselves as hermits near the
cave of Elias on Mount Carmel. About 1210 the hermits on Carmel
received from Albert, Latin Patriarch of Jerusalem, a rule comprising sixteen articles.

This was the primitive Carmelite rule. The life prescribed was
strictly eremetical: the monks were to live in separate cells or huts
devoted to prayer and work; they were to live a life of great silence,
seclusion, abstinence, and austerity. The rule received papal
approbation in 1226.

When Carmel became an unsafe place for the hermits, they
migrated first to Cyprus and then to Sicily, France, and England.

[101]   *Life*, 11-13.
[102]   Ibid., 14-15.
[103]   Ibid., 16-17.

impossible to read or speak; this lasts a bare half hour, but may lessen and return so as to occupy hours. The utmost point of transformation in God lasts only an instant. When the effects extend to the body, insensibility, ecstasy, rapture, or flight of the spirit is produced, and even levitation occurs.[104] Theresa speaks further of locutions[105] and of intellectual and imaginary visions.[106] She concludes with more purely mystical visions of the "truth itself" and how all things are in God.[107]

In her last work, *The Interior Castle*, she declares that it is a delusion when people think that they cannot meditate, however sublime their prayers may be; and in her work *Way of Perfection* she describes meditation as quite easy. Still later she realized that her view that meditation is easy was incorrect.

Known for her visions and efforts to bring about reforms in the Church so necessary at that time because of its low spiritual state, Theresa founded a very ascetic sisterhood known as *Descalzos* (Barefoots). She established and supervised sixteen convents and fourteen monasteries. Her work *The Way of Perfection* was adopted as a guidebook for nuns. Theresa was canonized in 1622.

Saint John of the Cross

St. John of the Cross (1542-1591) became a professed Carmelite in 1564. He is considered one of the greatest writers on mystical theology produced by the Roman Catholic Church.

---

[104]   Ibid., 18-20.
[105]   Ibid., 25.
[106]   Ibid., 27-29.
[107]   Ibid., 40.

Of his several books, his *Dark Night of the Soul, The Ascent of Mt. Carmel, The Living Flame,* and *The Spiritual Canticle* are among the greatest mystical treatises of all time.

Much of what St. John wrote about deals with the subjects of prayer and meditation. In relation to prayer, he refuses to estimate its effects upon the soul and body, as it brings peace and joy to the one and pain to the other. On the contrary, he tests all such manifestations by their influence on union with God, none of these psychical and psycho-physical phenomena is a proximate means of union, and the same is true of every sort of vision, locution, etc. None of these things is to be desired or prayed for, and, if they occur, they must not be attended to. It is not necessary, he states, even to decide whether visions and locutions are from God, from the imagination or from the devil; they are merely to be set aside and never thought of; by this means they can do no harm if they are not from God, while if they are divine, they will produce their due effect without our attending to them. All our effort is to be to attain union with God, with His will.

The lofty symbolism of St. John's prose is frequently obscure, but his lyrical verses are distinguished for their rapturous ecstasy and beauty of expression.

Jacob Boehme

The greatest of all early Protestant mystics was Jacob Boehme (1575-1624), born a few miles from Görlitz in Silesia.

Though an uneducated man, a shoemaker by trade, Boehme read much, and absorbed into his meditative and original mind many strands of earlier thought-systems.

The core of Boehme's message sprang out of his own deep experience and his own vivid apprehension of the meaning of Christianity as a way of life. In the year 1600, as in "a flash of lightning," he felt that "the gate of his soul opened" and that he saw and knew what no books could teach him. His insights are expressed by him in a series of books.

His main ideas are these. Behind the visible, material, temporal universe, there is an invisible, immaterial, eternal universe which is the *mother* of the one that we see.

Salvation is not the result of opinions, or belief in creeds, or of the performance of outward sacraments, or of membership in an outward Church; rather it is the result of an inward union of heart with the revealed life of God; it is the life of God brought to a personal, conscious expression in the life of a man, so that "the Lily-Twig" blossoms in a new, individual form.

William Law

In William Law (1686-1761) Protestant mysticism attained its most perfect expression. He shows throughout his life the influence of the English Platonists. But he early formed his mind directly upon the great models of mystical piety.

During the first creative period of his life, he wrote *Christian Perfection* (1726) and *A Serious Call to a Devout and Holy Life* (1729). In this time of his life he strongly followed the lives of the exponents of classical, medieval mysticism, with much emphasis on self-denial and negation. His two books represent the culmination in England of the type of Christianity embodied in the sermons of Johannes Tauler.

In the second period of his life, which began about

1733, Law became more deeply insightful and more conscious of a direct, inward relation with a universe of invisible reality.

During this period, Law wrote *The Spirit of Prayer* (1749), *The Spirit of Love* (1752), and *The Way to Divine Knowledge* (1752). These books represent the noblest English interpretation of Jacob Boehme's mystical message.

Mystics among the British Poets

From the beginning of the English Reformation to the present time, British poets have shown deep sympathy with and clear appreciation of mysticism. In the 17th century John Donne, George Herbert, and Henry Vaughan were strongly influenced by Platonism and by classical mysticism, and they all gave expression in their poetry to the intimate inner relation of the soul with God. In the 19th century, Wordsworth, Coleridge, Tennyson, and Browning, foremost among English poets, were mystical both in their own personal experiences and in their interpretations of the soul's deepest life. William Blake (1757-1827), deeply versed in the writings of Boehme and possessed of a peculiarly marked psychical disposition, was the most distinctly mystical poet of the 19th century in England, as Ralph Waldo Emerson was in America.

The Difference between Mystics of the Past
and the Present

The closing years of the 19th century and the opening years of the 20th century have been marked by a widespread popular revival of mysticism which has found expression in an extensive body of religious literature.

The present return to mysticism is, however, in marked contrast to the great periods of mysticism. In all those characteristically different movements the leaders and exponents were themselves luminous mystics who interpreted their own experiences. Today, on the other hand, very few firsthand prophets of mystical religion have appeared. The present movement has been, in the main, confined to the historical and psychological interpretation of mysticism as revealed in the autobiographies and expositions of mystics of the past. This may be, and probably is, the necessary preliminary stage to a far more profound return to religious mysticism.

Chapter VI

Islamic Mysticism

Mysticism is a belief in the
oneness of the universe.
S.U.

The Meaning of the Word *Sūfi*

 slamic mystics are known as "Sūfis."
There are several theories for the deriva-
tion and meaning of the term. Most Sūfis
favor the theory that it is derived from
safa ("purity") and that the Sūfi is one of
the elect who have become purified from
all worldly defilements. Others connect the word with
saff ("rank") as though the Sūfi were spiritually in the
first rank in virtue of his communion with God; or with
suffa ("bench"), referring the origin of Sūfism to the

Ahl al-suffia ("people of the bench"), a title given in the early days of Islam to certain poor Muslims who had no house or lodging and therefore used to take shelter on the covered bench outside the mosque built by the Prophet Mohammed. The author of the oldest extant Arabic treatise of Sūfism, Abū Nasr al-Sarrāj, declares that in his opinion the word "Sūfi" is derived from *sūf* ("wool"), for the woolen raiment is the habit of the prophets and the badge of the saints and elect in many traditions and narratives.[108]

The Koran and the Mystical Element

The Koran contains a few passages from which it can be argued that Mohammed had in him something of the mystic, even though the book as a whole can hardly be considered a basis for a system of mysticism. The Sūfis, however, adopting the Shiite principle of allegorical interpretation, were able to prove to their own satisfaction that every verse and word of the sacred text hides treasures of meaning which God reveals to the elect, meanings which flash upon the inward eye in moments of rapt meditation.[109]

So much being granted, one can imagine that it was easy to show Koranic authority for any mystical doctrine whatsoever. From the same principle it follows that the Sūfi interpretation of Islam admits an endless variety of divergent and even contradictory beliefs and practices, all of which are equally valid in kind though not in degree, since the meanings of the Koran are infinite and reveal themselves to each mystic in pro-

---

[108]   Abū Nasr al Sarrāj, *Kitab al-Luma*, ed. R.A. Nicholson (London: 1916), p. 20.

[109]   Ibid., p. 82.

portion to the spiritual capacity with which he is endowed. Hence the Sūfis are not to be regarded as a sect, for there is no uniform body of doctrine constituting what is called Sūfism. The many-sidedness of the term is exemplified by the innumerable attempts made to define it. Similarly, the attitude of the Sūfis toward Mohammed on religious law depends on subjective criteria. Some punctiliously fulfilled their ritual obligations, while at the same time they recognized that forms of worship have only a relative value in comparison with "the works of the heart," or are altogether worthless except as symbols of spiritual realities. Many Sūfis, however, insist that normally perfect realization of the Truth—i.e., the consummation of the mystical life—is not only compatible with the observance of the Law but includes it as a facet or aspect of the whole.

The Development of Islamic Mysticism

The germs of mysticism, latent in Islam from the first, rapidly developed in the two centuries following the prophet's death as a result of Messianic hopes and presages, the luxury of the upper classes, and the hard, mechanical piety of the Orthodox creed. The terrors of hell, so vividly depicted in the Koran, awakened in many an intense consciousness of sin, which drove them to seek salvation in ascetic practices. Before long the asceticism passed into mysticism,

In the evolution of Sūfism, influences outside of Islam made themselves powerfully felt. More than one Sūfi doctrine shows traces of Christian teachings. The monastic strain which insinuated itself into Sūfism in spite of Mohammed's prohibition was derived from

Christianity. Buddhism also had its influence on Sūfism. Buddhist monks carried their religious practices
and philosophy among the Muslims in countries which
were conquered by Mohammed. Another great foreign
influence on Sūfism was Neoplatonic philosophy.
Between 800 and 860 the tide of Greek learning, then at
its height, streamed into Islam. The so-called *Theology
of Aristotle*, which was translated into Arabic about
840, is full of Neoplatonic theories, and the mystical
writings of the pseudo-Dionysius were widely known
throughout western Asia.

By the end of the third century after Mohammed's
death, Sūfi mysticism was fast becoming an organized
system, with rules of discipline and devotion which the
novice was bound to learn from his spiritual director, to
whose guidance he submitted himself absolutely as to
one regarded as being in intimate communion with
God. During the next two hundred years (900-1100),
various manuals of theory and practice were compiled.
They all expatiate on the discipline of the soul and
describe the process of purgation which it must undergo
before entering the contemplative life.

The Illusion of Individuality

Islamic mysticism teaches that man's soul is of
divine origin; here on earth and in the body it is an
alien and in exile. The goal of the Islamic mystic, therefore, which is the same for any other mystic, is liberation from the body and from the world, return to God,
union with God—a union in which the finite personality is swallowed up and lost in the infinite and in losing
finds its true self. Individuality is no more than illusion. Since the illusion of individuality is produced by

the distinctive qualities or attributes of the individual, the aim of the mystic, therefore, is to rid himself of these.

This goal will not be achieved at once by an audacious bound into the bosom of the Infinite, but only by progressive stages in the path which has been marked by those who have already attained union and been made perfect. The Sūfi, therefore, calls himself a wayfarer on the road which leads to "the truth," the one Reality in the universe.

The Stages the Wayfarer Must Traverse

The stages that the wayfarer is expected to traverse before he can achieve his goal are: repentance, abstinence, renunciation, poverty, patience, trust in God, and satisfaction. The wayfarer must traverse these stages in succession, making himself perfect in each before proceeding to the next. These stages constitute the ascetic and ethical discipline of the Sūfi.

The first step in the stages, repentance, includes not only contrition for past sins against God or men, but the abandonment of them, with full resolve never again to repeat them, and reparation of the wrongs which one had done to his fellows.

The penitent seeker next puts himself under the guidance of a director, a man of experience and approved piety, whose injunctions he follows in everything. The probationary period is sometimes extended over a period of three years. In the first year the novice is bidden to devote himself to the service of his fellow men; in the second, to the service of God, and in the third, to watchfulness over his own thoughts. He can only serve his fellow men when he esteems all men better than himself; he can only serve God when he worships Him without regard to his own advantage in this life or the other; and he can only keep his own heart when his thoughts are collected and every care dismissed, so that he can commune with God without distraction. Only after the trial period is one permitted to assume the patched woolen garment which is the distinctive dress of the mystic.

The States Bestowed on the Mystic

Distinct from the stages are the states of the mystic, which are ten in number and which are not attainments of man but emotions and experiences which God bestows on man when and how he will. These "states" are: meditation, nearness to God, love, fear, hope, longing, intimacy, tranquility, contemplation, and certainty. They descend from God into man's heart without his being able to repel them when they come or retain them when they go.

When a man has traversed all the stages of the path and experienced whatever states God was pleased to bestow upon him, only then does he enter upon that higher plane of consciousness which the Sūfi calls Knowledge and Truth; only then does the seeker become the knower, in whom knower and knowing and known are identical.

This transcendental knowledge cannot be attained by the methods of sense or the speculations of philosophy, nor can it be imparted by teaching. It comes in a flash of intuition, or rather of divine illumination. Those who possess it cannot describe it, for the truth is inexpressible, inconceivable. It is at once self-knowledge and knowledge of God, for these are not two but one; the secret lies in the realization that the appearance of otherness is nought but illusion.

The ecstasy of this experience is often spoken of as intoxication—an exaltation and expansion in which the consciousness of self is surmounted. Still more often, as in the mystic poetry of all ages and religions, it is in the love of God that man loses himself and finds the fulfillment of his being. He who loves God supremely, the Sūfis maintain, sees God in all his creatures, and expresses this divine love in all his dealings with them.

The Goal of the Sūfi Path

The goal of the Sūfi path is not the intellectual intuition of oneness, but the emotional experience of it, the rapture of love in the possession of the beloved, or rather in being possessed by the beloved. This experience is presented in imagery borrowed from human love, not by way of intentional allegory but because it is the only language that is poetically possible. God is the perfection of beauty; it is this supreme beauty which inspires the mystic's love, and it is his love which enables him to see in God beauty to which other men are blind.

The Mystic's Love of God

Only by love is God known. Revelation, however true it may be, cannot give this knowledge, for revelation is a necessary accommodation to the incapacity of the common mind—at best, an attempt to say what cannot be expressed in words. It is equally futile to look for knowledge of God in the definitions and discussions of

philosophers and scholastic theologians. Love is also
the key to the understanding of God's dealings with
men. Why does God deal thus with men? Reason discovers no answer, revelation gives none; but he who
loves understands, as a child through love discerns the
benevolent motives of a father's severity, if not his wise
design.

The true servant of God is so lost in contemplation of
Him that he no longer attributes his own actions to
himself, but refers them all to God. One Sūfi poet, Jalal
al-Din Rumi, writes: "When the temporal joins itself to
the eternal, the former has no more existence. Thou
hearest and seest nought but Allah! When thou reach-
est the conviction that there is no existence except
Allah, when thou realizest that thou thyself are He,
that thou art identical with Him, then nothing exists
but He!"

> Let me become non-existent, for non-existence calls to
> me with organ tones, "To him we return!"[110]

A Sūfi by the name of Al-Hallaj was put to death in
922 A.D. for proclaiming himself in the city of Bagdad
as the true Reality—"Ana al-Hakk" ("I am the
Reality")—the sole Reality in the universe, God. What
Hallaj meant to say by his misunderstood outcry was
that his soul was merged with God. According to Hallaj, man is essentially divine. God created man in His
own image; He projected from Himself that image of
His eternal love that He might behold Himself as in a
mirror. Inasmuch as the humanity of God embraces
the whole bodily and spiritual nature of man, the divinity of God cannot unite with that nature except by an

---

[110]   N.H. Dole and Belle M. Walker, eds., *The Persian Poets* (New
York: Thomas Y. Crowell, 1901), p. 219.

incarnation or an infusion of the divine spirit such as
takes place when the human spirit enters the body.
Thus, Hallaj says in one of his poems:

> Thy spirit is mingled in my spirit,
> even as wine is mingled with pure water.
> When anything touches thee it touches me.
> Lo in every case thou art I![111]

And again:

> I am he whom I love, and he whom I love is I:
> We are two spirits dwelling in one body.
> If thou seest me, thou seest him,
> And if thou seest him, thou seest us both.[112]

It is evident from this that, in place of the one personal God, the creator of the world, the Sūfis put the
sole reality in the universe, the One, the Truth. And in
place of divine judgment, reward and punishment in
the future life, they put a mystical love in which lover
and beloved are one, or a transcendental knowledge of
identity in which the illusion of individuality is
overcome.

As in all similar systems, the positive elements of
religion, its commandments and observances, have no
meaning or value to him who has attained the truth.
Most of the Sūfis outwardly conformed to the religious
law and custom in order to avoid scandal and punishment, but there were some who held themselves eman-
cipated, not only in spirit, but from the letter of the law.
Antinomianism is, indeed, inherent in all mysticism.

The Sūfis applied to the Koran an allegorical method

---

[111]   R.A. Nicholson, *The Mystics of Islam* (Cambridge, England:
Cambidge University Press, 1930), p. 151.
[112]   Ibid., p. 151.

of interpretation by which they found beneath the surface a spiritual sense, and the more extreme among
them acknowledged no other significance in the Koran.
They were called the *Batiniyya*, which might literally
be translated as "Insiders"—that is, those who seek,
and find, the true inwardness of the teaching. For these
individuals the differences between religions disappear. The love of God, they believe, may be attained by
Jews or Christians as well as by Muslims.

Ibn Arabi says, "There was a time when I took it
amiss in my companion if his religion was not like
mine, but now my heart admits every form. It is a
pasture for gazelles, a cloister for monks, a temple for
idols, a Kaaba for the pilgrim, the tables of the Law,
and the sacred book of the Koran. Love alone is my
religion and whithersoever men's camels turn, it is my
religion and my faith."[113]

The conviction of the Sūfis that the essential thing in
religion—any religion—is religious experience ("the
inward spirit and the state of feeling"), rather than its
fixed forms, is reflected in the following passage in
Mathnavi by Rūmī:

> Moses saw a shepherd on the way, who was saying,
> "O God who choosest whom Thou wilt, where art Thou,
> that I may become Thy servant and sew Thy shoes and
> comb Thy head? That I may wash Thy clothes and kill
> Thy lice and bring milk to Thee, O worshipful One; that
> I may kiss Thy little hand and rub Thy little foot, and
> when bedtime comes I may sweep Thy little room, O
> Thou to whom all my goats be a sacrifice, O Thou in
> remembrance of whom are my cries of ay and ah!"
> The shepherd was speaking foolish words in this
> wise. Moses said, "Man, to whom is this addressed?"

---

[113] I. Goldziher, *Mohammed and Islam*, trans. K.C. Seelye (New
Haven: Yale University Press, 1917), p. 183.

He answered, "To that One who created us; by whom this earth and sky were brought to sight."

"Hark!" said Moses. "You have become very back-sliding: indeed you have not become a Moslem, you have become an infidel. What babble is this? What blasphemy and raving? Stuff some cotton into your mouth! The stench of your blasphemy has made the whole world stinking: your blasphemy has turned the silk robe of religion into rags. Shoes and socks are fitting for you, but how are such things right for One who is a Sun?"

The shepherd said, "O Moses, thou hast closed my mouth and thou hast burned my soul with repentance." He rent his garment and heaved a sigh, and hastily turned his head towards the desert and went his way.

A revelation came to Moses from God—"Thou hast parted My servant from me. Didst thou come as a prophet to unite, or didst thou come to sever? So far as thou canst, do not set foot in separation: of all things the most hateful to Me is divorce. I have bestowed on every one a special way of acting.... In the Hindus the idiom of India is praiseworthy; in the Sindians the idiom of Sind is praiseworthy. I am not sanctified by their glorification of Me; 'tis they that become sancti-fied.... I look not at the tongue and the speech; I look at the inward spirit and the state of feeling. I gaze into the heart to see whether it be lowly, though the words uttered be not lowly, because the heart is the sub-stance.... In substance is the real object. How much more of these phrases and conceptions and metaphors? I want burning, burning: become friendly with that burning! Light up a fire of love in thy soul, burn thought and expression entirely away! O Moses, they that know the conventions are of one sort, they whose souls and spirits burn are of another sort.[114]

---

[114]   John D. Yohannan, ed., *A Treasury of Asian Literature* (New York: Mentor Books, 1958), p. 31.

The Soul Seeking Its Source

An effort to present a philosophical and mystical
conception of reality appears in a collection of essays
by certain members of a society in Basra who call
themselves the *Ikhwan al-Safā*, the "Sincere Ones."
The essays are arranged in four divisions. The first
part deals with the fundamental sciences (arithmetic,
geometry, astronomy, geography, the theory of music,
mathematical relations) and logic; the second treats of
the natural sciences and of man; the third division is
devoted to the doctrine of the Universal Soul and the
relations of partial and of individual souls to it; the
fourth part concerns itself with the theological sciences. The first two parts and the last are in the main
Aristotelian: the doctrine of the soul is Platonic, but
with a considerable admixture of Pythagorian and
Aristotelian elements.

The Plotinian theory of emanations underlies the
whole. First is the One, the Absolute; then the Universal Intelligence; then the Universal Soul; the Primor-
dial Matter; and finally the world of things. Under the
influence of Pythagorean number mysticism, however,
these stages are by subdivision increased to nine. The
Universal Soul is one, but it has many powers, which
permeate all nature and which are distributed in all
bodies and elements, from the planets down to the
plants; these powers are what are called the souls of
these creatures, and, as in Plotinus, constitute a system
of souls in the Universal Soul. Man is a microcosm; and
the correspondence of his nature to the macrocosm is a
favorite theme of these writers. In the material world
and in union with the body, the soul is, as it were, in a
state of stupor, unmindful of its origin, its nature, and
its destiny. When it is awakened from its slumber, it
seeks to return to its source, the Universal Soul.

The Sūfi View of Resurrection

According to the Sūfis, resurrection is not to be understood as the re-creation of the body, but the awakening of the soul from its heedless slumber; it is the return from the world of matter and body to the world of spirit or of mind. The great resurrection is the separation of the Universal Soul from the material world and its return to God. Hell, in their view, is not a place of material torment where an angry God punishes sinners in the fire; the sinful soul, they believe, has its hell in its own body in this life.

Those who are awakened from the sleep of folly recognize the full value of things. To them every day is a festival, every moment an act of worship. All places and all times are alike to them; there is only one place of worship and that place is where one fulfills the word of God. Their love of God manifests itself in religious toleration and in kindliness toward all creatures; it gives those who possess it in this life composure of soul, heart-freedom, and peace with the whole world, and hereafter the ascent to the eternal light.

The Reconciliation of Sūfism with Sunnism

The accent by the mystics on the immanence and omnipresence of God was so at odds with the Sunni emphasis on the transcendence and omnipotence of God that there was great need of a reconciliation of these themes, and this need was met by al-Ghazzāli, the great synthesizer of Muslim thought.

Al-Ghazzāli was born in a Persian village in 1058; he attained his fame elsewhere but returned home before he died in 1111. After an education in jurisprudence in a *Shāfi'ite* school, and in theology under a famous

Asharite imām, he was invited to lecture at a newly founded university in Baghdad where the Asharite doctrine predominated. During his four years of teaching, he reached a spiritual crisis. Not satisfied with scholasticism, he veered to skepticism, then to Sūfism.

He left the university, and went to Syria to find out for himself, under the Sūfis there, whether their way was the right path to religious certainty. After two years of meditation and prayer he made a holy pilgrimage to Mecca before returning to his wife and children. He had renewed his faith in the Sunni ideal, but he felt that Sūfi mysticism, moderately practiced, could help him reach it. He began writing. Though at the command of the sultan he returned to teaching for a short time, he soon resumed his meditation and writing in his native village until his death at fifty-three.

His greatest book was *The Revivification of the Religious Sciences*. As a fundamentally religious person, he was not satisfied with the legalism and intellectualism of the Sunnis. He took the time to analyze in detail the philosophies of certain Muslim followers of Aristotle, only to condemn them as self-contradictory, and essentially irreligious, rational systems. To him the universe was not eternal but was created out of nothing by the creative will of Allah. The relation between men and the great being who has produced them and the world about them should be fundamentally moral and experiental. It is not enough to observe the laws and rites of Islam or to have a *kalām* that one is ready to defend against all comers.

A humble soul may be profoundly religious even though he be ignorant of the details of Koranic interpretation or theology. The core of religion—which may be practiced even by a non-Muslim—is to repent of one's sins, purge the heart of all but God, and by the exercises of religion attain a virtuous character. And here, he said, the Sūfi methods of self-discipline and meditation, if practiced with common sense and wisdom, are of great value.

The vigor with which al-Ghazzāli censured the teachers of law, theology, and philosophy for their lack of religious fire and for encouraging sectarian tendencies caused his works to be bitterly assailed when they were first published. But as time went on all but the more extreme sects in areas dominated by formalistic jurisprudence, such as far-off Spain, acknowledged the sanity and general truth of his position. Ultimately, he was called the greatest Muslim thinker, and was at last revered as a saint. And just as Catholic schoolmen have not gone far from the positions of Aquinas, so Muslim thinkers have remained in the main content with al-Ghazzāli's formulations, his word being taken as all but final.

Sūfi Poetry with Mystical Meaning

In Sūfi poetry the meaning is mystical but the form is sensuous. Unless we have some clue from the writer, it is not easy to determine whether we are reading an ode of human love or a hymn addressed to the Deity.[115] Should it be asked why the Sufi poets employ so much erotic symbolism, the answer is that they could find no analogy more suggestive and better adapted to show forth the states of enthusiasm and ecstasy which they describe.

Wine, torch, and beauty are epiphanies of Verity,
For it is that which is revealed under all forms soever.
Wine and torch are the transport and light of the knower;
Behold the Beauty, for it is hidden from none.

---

[115] Nicholson, *The Mystics of Islam*, p. 102.

Wine, torch, and beauty all are present;
Neglect not to embrace that Beauty
Quaff the wine of dying to self, and for a season
Peradventure you will be freed from the dominion of self.
Drink wine, for its cup is the face of the Friend;
The flagon is His eye drunken and flown with wine.[116]

God, as the poets conceive him, is the eternal Beauty which by the necessity of its nature desires to be loved, manifests itself for the sake of love, and is the real object of all love. Even earthly love is a spiritual type, a bridge leading to reality. The soul, being divine in its essence, longs for union with that from which it is separated by the illusion of individuality; and this aspiration of longing, which urges it to pass away from selfhood and to rise on the wings of ecstasy is the only means whereby it can return to its original home. Love transmutes into pure gold the base phenomenal alloy of which every creature partakes. While reason is dualistic, love unifies by transcending thought.

> The more a man loves, the deeper he penetrates the divine purposes. Love is "the astrolabe of heavenly mysteries," the eye-salve which clears the spiritual eye and makes it clairvoyant.[117]

Evil and Predestination through the Mystical Eyes of the Sūfi Poets

Through love we can discern, sing the Sūfi poets, that

---

[116]   E. H. Whinfield, ed. and trans., *Gulshani Raz* (London, 1880), p. 78.

[117]   E.H. Whinfield, *Masnavi-i Ma'navi: The Spiritual Couplets of Maulana Jalalu-'d-din Muhammad-i Rumi* (London, 1898), p. 28.

evil, so far as it has any real existence—and in relation
to God it has none—is a good in disguise or, at the
worst, a necessary condition for the manifestation of
good.

Regarding predestination, the poets maintain that
perfect love implies identity of will, and thus abolishes
the conflict between freedom and necessity.

The lyric poetry of Sūfism reaches its highest rank of
pantheistic hymns describing the states of *fanā* (negation of individuality) and *baqā* (affirmation of universal consciousness).

> Lo, for I to myself am unknown,
>   now in God's name what must I do?
> I adore not the Cross nor the Crescent,
>   I am not a Giaour nor a Jew.
> East nor West, land nor sea is my home,
>   I have kin nor with angel nor gnome,
> I am wrought not of fire nor of foam,
>   I am shaped not of dust nor dew,
> I was born not in China afar, not in
>   Saqsin not in Bulghar;
> Not in India, where five rivers are,
>   nor Iraq nor Khorasan I grew.
> Not in this world nor that world I
>   dwell, not in Paradise, neither in Hell,
> Not from Eden and Rizwan I fell, not
>   from Adam my lineage I drew.
> In a place beyond uttermost Place,
>   in a tract without shadow of trace,
> Soul and body transcending I live in
>   the soul of my Loved One anew![118]

---

[118] R.A. Nicholson, *Selected Poems from the Divani Shamsi
Tabriz* (Cambridge, 1898), p. 344.

The Sūfi poems were largely composed under the influence of ecstasy and are in fact analogous to what is now known as automatic writing. Their rhythm and melody, combined with the symbolic form in which they are clothed, give them the strange power of communicating to the reader the same feeling of rapture by which their composers were inspired.

Conclusion

an is a two-faceted being. He is a composition of matter and spirit. The material aspect of him draws him to the phenomenal world, the world of the senses, which titillates him with its promises of a life of satisfaction and security.

The spiritual aspect of him draws him to the source of his origin, the "Over Soul," and guarantees him inner freedom and inner peace.

These two aspects of the human being are constantly at odds within him. Each is clamoring for his fullest attention.

Those who lavish their attention on the material life discover sooner or later that, no matter how much they acquire of things material, they remain unsatisfied. They are endlessly driven to get more and more things hoping that their hunger for them will eventually be quelled. But this does not happen, so their pursuit of these things continues. These individuals are known as materialists.

At the other extreme are those who give their undivided attention to the life of the spirit. They view the material world as unreal, illusory. Only that which the spirit leads them to they claim to be real. Those whose lives are governed by this outlook are called mystics.

Before man can ever know true Reality, the mystics affirm, he must first transcend the sense world, turn a deaf ear to its cry for material things, escape its bondage, and be reborn to a higher level of consciousness. He must shift his center of interest from the material to the spiritual plane. According to the thoroughness with which he does this will he experience true Reality.

But if man were to turn his back on the material life and sink instead into the life of the spirit, human life on earth would fall into a state of rest. Creativity would cease. The human intellect would deteriorate. Civilization would stop its onward march.

Now, which should be the goal for man to pursue? Which voice is he to heed, the voice of matter or the voice of the spirit? This question may arise in one's mind after reading this book. The answer to the question, by virtue of man's composition, is that he must give heed to both voices.

By recognizing the importance of both aspects of his being, by attempting to satisfy the need of both, man is bound to attain balance in his life. The reward for such an achievement has been proven to be a life of love, security, and serenity.

Glossary

Allah (*uhl-laah*). The Koranic term for the one true God.

Amitabha (*aa-mu-tha-bha*). Widely honored throughout the east as a savior Buddha.

Apocrypha (*uh-poc-ru-fuh*). Books excluded from some versions of the Bible as not authoritative.

arhat (*aarh-huht*). One who is following various disciplines leading to enlightenment, usually a monk in the Theravada tradition.

Atman (*aaht-mun*). Self, or soul and Self, or Soul of the universe.

Ba-al (*baa-uhl*). Storm God of the ancient Canaanites. In Hebrew the term means "master."

bhakti (*bhuhk-ti*). Devotion to a god; devotional practices.

bodhi (*boh-dhee*). Enlightenment.

bodhisattva (*boh-dhu-suh-tvuh*). One who has attained enlightenment.

Brahman (*bruh-muhn*). The Source of the Universe or Ultimate Reality.

185

Brahman-atman (*bruh-muhn at-muhn*). The unity of the self with Absolute reality.

Brahmanas (*braah-muhn-us*). Vedic commentaries on the ritual.

cenobite (*sen-oh-bite*). One in a religious order who lives within a community and maintains vows of silence.

dhyana (*dhu-yaa-nuh*). Contemplation, meditation in the practice of yoga.

dhyani Buddhas (*dhu-yaa-nih-Buddhas*). Buddhas who have achieved Buddhahood as cosmic spirits without human manifestation.

eremite (*eh-reh-mite*). One who lives the life of a hermit.

Essenes. An ascetic Jewish sect in the 2nd and 1st centuries B.C.

Hasidism. "Pietism," from *Hasid* ("pious"), a mystical movement founded in the 18th century in Eastern Europe by Israel Ba-al Shem Tov. Hasidism may be considered to be an outgrowth of the Kabbala.

jnana (*jnaah-nuh*). A form of knowledge.

Kabbala (*kab-baah-luh*). Medieval mystical movement based on older mystical traditions.

karma (*kahr-muh*). The belief that one's present condition is due to his own past deeds.

Karuna (*kuh-roo-nuh*). An attitude of compassion found in Buddhas and Bodhisattvas which is to be emulated by Buddhists.

Logos. Word, the Divine word, the chief instrument of God's creative activity, regarded in the Christian tradition as having been incarnated in Jesus.

Metatron (*met-taat-ruhn*). A term for the highest angel or archangel.

Midrash (*meed-raash*). Expositions of Biblical texts to bring out legal precepts and ethical principles. Also "inquiry" into the meaning of Torah passages or words—a basis for a sermon.

Neshamah (*ne-shuh-muh*). Soul.

Nirvana (*nir-vah-nuh*). The "snuffing out" of the fires of life, which brings release from rebirth and a sublime calm and peace.

Prajapati (*praj-aah-pahthi*). "Lord of creatures," a creator god in late Vedic tradition.

Sakyamuni (*saa-kyuh-mun-nee*). A name of the original, historical Buddha which means "risen one of the Sakya [clan]."

Samsara. The transmigration of the human soul.

Sanskrit. The language of the Vedic Aryans and of classical Hinduism. It is the basis of most North Indian languages.

Sepher Yetzirah. The Book of Creation or Formation.

Sefiroth. Name given in Kabbala to the ten creative powers—arranged in a gradation from the most spiritual to the least, through which the divine original Essence manifests itself in the world.

skandhas (*skuhn-daahs*). The aggregate or constituent elements in personality, which are five in number: body, feelings or sensations, perceptions, habitual tendencies, and consciousness.

Sūfi (*soo-fee*). "Wool weaver," a Muslim who seeks through the path of religious experience and spiritual discipline to acquire intimacy with God.

Sunni (*sun-nee*). The term used to designate a group in Islam called the *ahlal Sunna w'al Jama'a*, the people of the tradition and the majority.

transmigration. The movement of the soul at death from one life to the next. In India the view that human existence is an unending series of earthly lives, with the soul transmigrating from one to the next, has always been linked with the idea of karma and the religious quest has been an effort to find a way of escape from this chain of continuing existences.

trikaya (*trih-kaa-yuh*). The three bodies of the Buddha:
nirmankaya, visible body; *sambhogokaya*, the body
of bliss; and *dharmakaya*, body of truth.

tripitaka (*trih-pih-taka*). The baskets of Buddhists'
sacred texts: *Vinaya Pitaka*, Discipline Basket (for
monks); *Sutta Pitaka*, Discourse Basket; and
Abbudhama Pitaka, Basket of Special Teachings.

Upanishads (*u-puh-ni-shuds*). The last of the Vedic
scriptures, collection of dialogues, stories, and teachings, some of which are philosophical in character.

Vedas (*vay-duhs*). The most ancient and sacred Hindu
scriptures.

Vishnu (*vish-nu*). One of the two greatest gods of
Hinduism.

Yoga (*yoh-guh*). The way of salvation through inner
discipline—for developing sources of insight.

Yogi (*yoh-gee*). A person who practices the discipline of
Yoga.

Zohar. "Splendor," brightness, derived from Daniel
12:3. A Jewish mystical work which became the
classic text of the Kabbala.

Bibliography

CHAPTER I

Bergson, Henri. *The Creative Mind.* New York: Philosophical Library, 1946.

Butler, Dom. C. *Western Mysticism.* London: Constable, 1927.

Herman, E. *The Meaning and Value of Mysticism.* London, 1907.

Inge, William R. *Mysticism in Religion.* Chicago: University of Chicago Press, 1948.

Jones, Rufus. *Studies in Mystical Religion.* London: Macmillan, 1923.

Leuba, J.H. *The Psychology of Religious Mysticism.* New York: Harcourt Brace, 1926.

Patmore, Coventry. *The Rod, the Root, and the Flower.* 2nd ed. London, 1907.

Royce, Josiah. *The World and the Individual.* New York: Macmillan, 1927.

Scharfstein, Ben Ami. *Mystical Experience.* New York: Penguin Books, 1974.

Smith, Margaret. *An Introduction to Mysticism.* New York: University Press, 1977.

Stace, Walter T. *Mysticism and Philosophy.* Philadelphia: Lippincott, 1960.

———. *The Teaching of the Mystics.* New York: New American Library, 1960.

Underhill, Evelyn. *Mysticism.* New York: E.P. Dutton, 1911.

Waite, Arthur E. *Lamps of Western Mysticism.* New York: Multimedia, 1963.

Watkin, Edward I. *The Philosophy of Mysticism.* London: Grant Richards, 1920.

Zaehner, R.C. *Mysticism: Sacred and Profane.* Oxford: Oxford University Press, 1957.

CHAPTER II

Bloomfield, Maurice. *The Religion of the Veda.* New York: G.P. Putnam's Sons, 1908.

De Bary, William Theodore, ed. *Sources of Indian Tradition.* New York: Columbia University Press, 1958.

Deussen, Paul. *Philosophy of the Upanishads.* New York: Dover Publishers, 1966. Originally published in 1906.

Embree, Ainslee T., ed. *The Hindu Tradition.* Westminster, Maryland: Random House, 1972.

Griswold, H.D. *The Religion of the Rig-Veda.* Oxford: Oxford University Press, 1923.

Hastings, James, ed. *Encyclopedia of Religion and Ethics.* Rev. ed. New York: Charles Scribner's Sons, 1955-58.

Hopkins, Thomas. *The Hindu Religious Tradition.* Encino, California: Dickenson Publishing Co., 1971.

Hume, Robert E., trans. *The Thirteen Principal Upani-*

shads. Rev. ed. London: Oxford University Press, 1962.

Keith, A.B. *The Religion and Philosophy of the Veda and the Upanishads*. Cambridge, Massachusetts: Harvard University Press, 1920.

Parrinder, Geoffrey. *Mysticism in the World's Religions*. New York: Oxford University Press, 1976.

Radhakrishnan, S. *The Philosophy of the Upanishads*. London: George Allen and Unwin, 1924.

Stutley, Margaret and James. *Harper's Dictionary of Hinduism*. New York: Harper and Row, 1977.

Walker, Benjamin. *The Hindu World, an Encyclopedic Survey of Hinduism*. New York: Praeger Publishers, Inc., 1968.

Zaehner, Richard C. *Hinduism*. New York: Oxford University Press, 1962.

Zimmer, Heinrich R. *Philosophies of India*. Edited by J. Campbell. New York: Meridian, 1956.

CHAPTER III

Blofeld, John. *Beyond the Gods: Buddhist and Taoist Mysticism*. New York: Dutton, 1974.

Conze, Edward. *Buddhism, Its Essence and Development*. New York: Philosophical Library, 1951.

Davids, T.W. Rhys, tr. *Dialogues to Buddha* (London: Oxford University Press, 1899-1921).

Eliot, Charles. *Japanese Buddhism*. New York: Barnes and Noble Books, 1959.

Hamilton, C.H. *Buddhism, a Religion of Infinite Compassion*. New York: Liberal Arts Publishers, 1952.

Kapleau, Philip. *The Three Pillars of Zen*. New York: Beacon Publishers, 1967.

Morgan, Kenneth W., ed. *The Path of Buddha*. New York: The Ronald Press Company, 1956.

Poussin, Louis DeLaVallee. *The Way to Nirvana*. Cambridge, England: Cambridge University Press, 1917.

Reischauer, A.K. *Studies in Japanese Buddhism*. New York: The Macmillan Company, 1917.

Robinson, Richard H. *The Buddhist Religion, a Historical Introduction*. Belmont, Cal., Dickenson Publishing Company, 1970.

Suzuki, Beatrice (Lane). *Impressions of Mahayana Buddhism*. Kyoto: Eastern Buddhist Society, 1940.

Suzuki, Daisetz Teitaro. *Essays in Zen Buddhism*. London: Rider, 1949.

CHAPTER IV

Abelson, J. *Jewish Mysticism*. London: G. Bell and Sons, 1913.

———. *The Immanence of God in Rabbinical Literature*. London, 1912.

Bennet, Charles A. *Philosophical Study of Mysticism*. New Haven, 1931.

Bension, Ariel. *The Zohar in Moslem and Christian Spain*. London, 1932.

Blumenthal, David R. *Understanding Jewish Mysticism*. New York: Ktav Publishing House, 1975.

Buber, Martin. *Jewish Mysticism and the Legends of the Baalshem*. Translated by Lucy Cohn. London, 1931.

Drummond, James. *Philo Judaeus*. London, 1888.

Fuller, J.F.C. *The Secret Wisdom of the Qabalah*. London, 1937.

Gaster, Moses. *The Origin of the Kabbala*. London: Judith Montefiore College, 1893-4.

Ginsburg, Christian D. *The Essenes, Their History and Doctrines*. London, 1864.

_____. *The Kabbalah: Its Doctrines, Development and Literature.* London, 1865.

Hertz, J.H. *Mystic Currents in Ancient Israel, Rise and Development of Cabala.* London, 1938.

Jones, Rufus M. *Studies in Mystical Religion.* London, 1909.

Mordell, Ph. "The Origin of Letters and Numbers according to the Sepher Yesira." *The Jewish Quarterly Review* 2: 557-83; 3: 517-44.

Muller, Ernst. *History of Jewish Mysticism.* Oxford: Phaidon Publishers Ltd., 1946.

Newman, Louis I., and Spitz, Sam. *Hasidic Anthology: Tales and Teachings of the Hasidim.* New York, London: Charles Scribner's Sons, 1935.

Philo Judaeus. *The Contemplative Life.* Edited by F.C. Conybeare. Oxford, 1896.

Schechter, Solomon. *The Chasidim: Studies in Judaism,* vol. 1. Philadelphia: Jewish Publication Society, 1896.

Scholem, Gershom G. *Major Trends in Jewish Mysticism.* Jerusalem: Schocken Publishing House, 1941.

Waite, A.E. *The Holy Kabbala.* London, 1927.

_____. *The Secret Doctrine in Israel: A Study of the Zohar and Its Connections.* London, 1913.

Wescott, William Wynn. *Sefer Yetzirah, the Book of Formation,* Bath, 1887.

Wolfson, Harry A. *Philo: Foundations of Religious Philosophy in Judaism, Christianity, and Islam.* Cambridge: Harvard University Press, 1948.

CHAPTER V

Augustine of Hippo. *The Confessions.* Translated by Dr. E.B. Pusey. London, 1907.

Battenhouse, R.W., ed. *A Companion to the Study of St. Augustine.* Oxford: Oxford University Press, 1955.

Butler, Dom Cuthbert. *Western Mysticism*. London, 1919.

Dyson, W.H. *Studies in Christian Mysticism*, 1913.

Eckhart, Meister. *Sermons*. Translated by C. de B. Evans. London, 1924.

Fleming, W.K. *Mysticism in Christianity*, 1913.

Granger, F.G. *The Soul of a Christian*. London, 1900.

Grant, Robert M. *Gnosticism: Source Book of Heretical Writings from the Early Christian Period*. New York: A.M.S. Press, 1961.

———. *Gnosticism and Early Christianity*. New York: Columbia University Press, 1966.

Gregory, Eleanor C. *An Introduction to Christian Mysticism*. London, 1901.

Inge, W.R. *Christian Mysticism*. London, 1899.

Jones, Rufus M. *Studies in Mystical Religion*. London, 1909.

Kelly, J.N.D. *Early Christian Doctrines*. New York: Harper and Brothers, Inc., 1958.

Pegis, A.C., ed. *Basic Writings of St. Thomas Aquinas*. New York: The Modern Library, 1948.

Plotinus. *The Enneads*, trans. by Stephen MacKenna. London, 1917-24.

Royce, Josiah. *The World and the Individual*. London, 1900.

Seesholtz, Anna Groh. *The Friends of God: Practical Mystics of the Fourteenth Century*. New York: A.M.S., 1934.

Spencer, Sidney. *Mysticism in World Religion*. South Brunswick, N.J.: A.S. Barnes and Co., Inc., 1963.

Tauler, John. *History and Life*. Translated by Susanna Winkworth. London, 1906.

Underhill, Evelyn. *The Mystics of the Church*. London, 1911.

Walters, Clifton, trans. *The Clouds of the Unknowing*. Baltimore: Penguin Books, 1961.

Wulf, M. de. *Scholasticism Old and New.* Dublin, 1907.

CHAPTER VI

Ali, Amir. *The Spirit of Islam.* London: Christopher's Ltd., 1922.

Arberry, A.J. *Sufism.* London: George Allen and Unwin, 1950.

Cragg, K. *Islam from Within.* Belmont: Wadsworth Publishing Company, 1979.

Dawood, N.J., trans. *The Koran.* 4th rev. ed. New York: Penguin Books, 1974.

Encyclopedia of Islam. Rev. ed. Leiden: E.J. Brill, 1960.

Fakhry, M. *History of Islamic Philosophy.* New York: Columbia University Press, 1974.

Gibb, H. *Mohammedanism.* Oxford: Oxford University Press, 1970.

Goldziher, I. *Mohammed and Islam.* Translated by K.C. Seelye. New Haven: Yale University Press, 1917.

Guillaume, Alfred. *Islam.* New York: Penguin Books, 1954.

Ibn Ishaq. *The Life of Muhammad.* Translated by A. Guillaume. London: Oxford University Press, 1955.

Lings, Martin. *What is Sufism?* London: George Allen and Unwin Ltd., 1975.

Nicholson, R.A. *The Mystics of Islam.* Cambridge, England: Cambridge University Press, 1930.

———. *Studies in Islamic Mysticism.* Cambridge, England: Cambridge University Press, 1921.

Schimmel, A. *Mystical Dimensions of Islam.* Chapel Hill: University of North Carolina Press, 1976.

Smith, Margaret. *The Sufi Path of Love.* Luzac & Co., 1954.

Smith, W. Robertson. *Religion of the Semites.* Cambridge, England: Cambridge University Press, 1885.

Tritton, A.S. *Muslim Theology*. Luzac & Co., 1947.
Williams, J.A. *Islam*. New York: Mentor Books, Inc., 1961.

Index